INDOOR PLANT HACKS 101

EASY TIPS, TRICKS, & DIYS TO DEVELOP YOUR GREEN THUMB AND KEEP YOUR HOUSEPLANTS THRIVING

MICHE FERRET

CONTENTS

INTRODUCTION

Ever heard of the term "green thumb"? Let's start with busting that myth for good. There's no such thing as a natural-born tendency to have more success with plants. If anything, you could intentionally develop a so-called "green thumb" by becoming more knowledgeable about different types of plants, their specific needs, and actually taking better care of them. It's the same with everything else; the more you learn and practice, the better results you yield (or, the greener your thumb gets).

As a kid, I remember planting pomegranate seeds — precisely 10 of them together (rookie mistake, I know) — in a corner of our backyard in hopes of growing an infinite supply of my favorite fruit. I dug out a little scoop of soil, gently placed my seeds in there, and covered it up. Sprinkled some water on top and hoped for the best, essentially relying on my green fingers to bear fruit. I even stuck up a little twig to help me remember where I planted my seeds. Spoiler alert: nothing happened — yep, shocker.

Fast forward to now. Having spent enough years as a genuine gardening fanatic, I've learnt that being a successful plant parent isn't hard — it just requires a certain sense of responsibility. You also need some know-how about the plants you plan on growing to make sure your dedication doesn't go to waste, which is exactly what this book is for.

I learned early on that growing plants is serious business and your success doesn't rely on luck. That's not a bad thing though, because it means there's no need to feel hopeless whenever you see one of your plants yellowing or dying. There's always something you can do or change to flip the script depending on the situation you're working with.

If you've been struggling with your houseplants' upkeep so far, you're not alone. In fact...

THE AVERAGE PLANT PARENT HAS KILLED SEVEN PLANTS

This stat comes from a OnePoll study conducted on houseplants and their millennial parents which found that the average parent was "guilty" of killing seven houseplants on average. A majority of them even call themselves "plant murderers" since most of the plants only started to deteriorate in health after being brought home from the nursery. They reported that some of their biggest worries as plant parents were making sure their plants were getting enough sunlight and water, and just keeping them alive and well in general. They were also concerned about stressing out the plant too much while relocating and looking for a reliable plant sitter on travel days.

Unfortunately, these innocent plant deaths generally stem (no pun intended) from a lack of awareness rather than carelessness on the parent's part. Most people still think they just need to regularly water their plants, keep them in a sunny place, and that's it. But even when they do so, some plants still die — leaving you in a state of disbelief, disappointment, and guilt. That's because sure, every plant needs water, sun, and soil to survive — but there's a lot more to it than just that. I believe seeking and applying just a little more accurate knowledge about plant care could prevent 99% of plant deaths that occur at the hands of newbies. And that's why I'm writing this book.

Every chapter of "**Indoor Plant Hacks 101**" will lay out the simplest, bite-sized chunks of information that'll wildly boost your success rates with different types of plants. These tips are golden nuggets that I've gathered over my years (or should I say, decades) of experience as a plant enthusiast, ever since I was just a little girl growing up in Miami.

Luckily, you don't have to spend that much time to be a house-plant pro. I'll take you there with just this book. And trust me, it'll all be worth it once you finally start to reap the benefits of having healthy houseplants thriving in your home!

5 OF MY FAVORITE HOUSEPLANT BENEFITS

Here are a few benefits that make my life just a little better everyday:

- **Better air quality:**

You gotta breathe, right? Houseplants are like natural air purifiers, which means they can help to remove toxins and pollutants from the air you breathe. Plus, they release oxygen and absorb carbon dioxide, making the air in your home fresher and healthier.

- **Reduced stress:**

Life can be stressful, but houseplants can help you relax. Studies have shown that simply looking at plants can reduce anxiety and lower your blood pressure, so having them around can help you feel more relaxed and at ease.

- **Increased productivity:**

Whether you work from home or just want to get stuff done around the house, having houseplants can boost your brain power. They've been shown to improve concentration, memory retention, and cognitive function, so you can stay focused and get more done — about 15% more.

- **Improved mood:**

Feeling down? Houseplants can help with that, too. Caring for plants can be therapeutic and provide a sense of purpose and accomplishment, which can make you feel happier and more fulfilled.

- **Aesthetic appeal:**

Finally, plants just look cool. They come in all sorts of shapes, sizes, and colors, so you can find ones that fit your personal style and add some natural beauty to your living space.

If you've deprived yourself of all these wonderful rewards of healthy houseplants, this book will finally change that. With all the hacks shared in the following chapters, your next batch of houseplants is bound to be a success story!

1

THE JOYS OF INDOOR PLANTS

P lants offer way more than just an aesthetic boost to your home. They can make your entire space come alive, giving you fresher air to breathe, and a healthier, more peaceful environment for you and your family to dwell in. Countless researches have shown how spending time in nature can boost mental health and many other aspects of physical well-being. But, in today's day and age, most of us sorely lack that aspect. Luckily, bringing some nature into your home can somewhat help counteract that.

It's easy to forget that they're actually alive — just like your pets! In fact, did you know that they LOVE listening to music? Feel free to plug those headphones out because research has shown that classical or jazz music encourages plants to grow faster. Metal music, on the other hand, induces stress though — so blasting your playlist out might not be a good idea if that's the genre you're into.

I love how plants give back so generously to reward you for keeping them happy and healthy. According to research, they have a calming effect that can keep you relaxed, improve your sleep quality, and reduce stress. And that's something we all need nowadays!

Aside from purifying and oxygenating your air, did you know that plants can even reduce noise pollution? Peace lilies, for instance, can absorb sound! So, feel free to have some of these around your workspace to boost your focus and productivity!

There's countless other stuff I could talk about here, but let's not get carried away. The point is, indoor plants are abundantly beneficial — and the best part is that they're not even hard to take care of as long as you know what you're doing.

FUN FACTS ABOUT HOUSEPLANTS

Here are some surprising facts about house plants that'll make you fall in love with this hobby all over again!

1. They enjoy company

Houseplants, just like humans, also prefer to have company around. When you cluster a few of them together, they mutually benefit thanks to the boost in humidity which comes from the moisture in their soil. As more moisture gets added into the air, your skin and sinuses will also thank you for it!

2. They respond to the way they're touched

Plant lovers have always felt so spiritually, but now science has also found evidence to back it — plants really can feel our touch and they even respond to it! Different types of sensations can cause them to develop genetic and physiological changes depending on the type of stimulus they're exposed to on a consistent basis. From a loving pat to some raindrops or dew, all these sensations seem to trigger unique responses.

3. They're fine with being home alone

Many new plant parents are quick to worry about finding plant sitters whenever they're planning a vacation week. Turns out, it's not that big of a deal — but this does depend on the type of plants you've got. Most of them, however, would do just fine if you pulled them away to a spot that doesn't get direct sunlight. As long as you're back in a week or so, you don't have to worry about coming home to dead or dying plants.

But with that said, you can't get careless about it. Be sure to at least space out these periods of isolation as houseplants do in fact depend on you for their well-being. For instance, absence of humans could result in a lack of CO_2 which isn't ideal for photosynthesis, potentially stunting their growth. While you're away, you won't be able to water them or adjust their positioning for adequate light sustenance. The plant will eventually notice the lack of care and it'll start to show signs if things don't go back to normal soon enough.

4. They grow better around human voices

Here's another adorable reason why I love plants so much. They're not the only ones doing you favors by purifying your air and enriching it with oxygen. They need you just as much! For instance, aside from your breathing being a source of CO_2 for them, even your voice could encourage plants to grow taller. This astonishing finding comes from a 2009 study by the RHS Royal Horticultural Society) which saw tomato plants growing noticeably taller upon being spoken to.

Who knew plants were incredible listeners as well? Feel free to vent out to your little green buddies after a long day at work!

5. Most common houseplants came from the tropics

Ever wondered how (or why) houseplants acclimate to living under the shade of your home or office roof so well? Well, that's partly because most species of houseplants come from subtropical or tropical origins where they grow under the enormous canopies of towering trees!

6. Growing plants indoors began in ancient times

The hobby of growing houseplants isn't anything new. The practice dates back to ancient times with Chinese, Egyptian, and Indian civilizations potting them for decorative, medicinal, or even recreational purposes.

But the practice wasn't always so common, though. It gained more traction during the 17th century after Sir Hugh Platt, famed agriculture author, wrote about cultivating several houseplants at home. Greenhouses and glasshouses started to be built shortly afterwards in England and surrounding areas to showcase gorgeous-looking exotic plants.

7. Indoor plants remove air pollution and allergens

Some people refuse to have houseplants because of "the mess" they make by dropping their leaves and whatnot. Well, there's some weight to that argument since plants can't really clean up after themselves. But, the benefits far outweigh that little caveat — in my opinion at least.

You see, plants are incredible at cleaning the air inside your house. They remove volatile compounds from the atmosphere which often exude from printers, furniture, paints, cleaning products, and even dry-cleaned clothes. All of those sources are ones that you can easily find inside a regular household or office. Such compounds are toxic and being exposed to them long-term can have serious respiratory and general health implications.

Aside from clearing out the CO_2 in the air, plants are also efficient in processing other gasses required during photosynthesis. Just by sitting in a corner of your home, plants will passively get rid of potentially harmful gasses which improves your indoor air quality. Even a medium-sized plant can absorb up to 25% toxins from the air of your room!

8. Office plants reduce stress

Stress… Something we're all a bit too well-versed with living in the 21st century. From studies and struggling with social media beauty standards, to managing work and parenting woes — nobody's safe from stress. In fact, it's been classified as "The Health Epidemic of the 21st century" by the World Health Organization WHO.

This means we need all the help we can get in fighting against it. Plants, fortunately, present a simple solution! According to studies, simply spending time looking at nature (rather than urban stuff) can bring down stress levels and have a significant positive influence on our mental well-being. Plus, breathing cleaner air can also mitigate stress by reducing your exposure to indoor contaminant compounds. Now, according to ABC, people living in the city spend about 90% of their time in indoor environments. Since houseplants can make such a big impact on how healthy those environments are for you, becoming a plant parent is pretty much a no-brainer decision.

9. They make your work zone more welcoming

One study performed in the UK and Netherlands showed that simply bringing in plants to a working environment brought productivity up by 15%. Professor Haslam — one of the authors credited for the study — suggested "Office landscaping helps the workplace become a more enjoyable, comfortable and profitable place to be."

According to another notable US study, about 10% of sick leaves can be caused by triggers like a lack of natural light in the office. It further shows how simply being around more natural beauty can positively affect our mood and self-esteem. And we all know that the happier you are, the more productive you can expect yourself to be!

10. Plants reduce noise levels

Air pollution is one thing, but did you know that plants even bring down noise pollution? If you're like me, you love your peace and quiet while working. Well, plants can play a helpful role by absorbing and reducing some of that background noise. To use this to full effect, research suggests it's best to position your largest plant pots in the corner and edges of a room. You could even install a floral centerpiece if you've got room for it. If you're pleased with the effects, why not use some of that desk space for small pots too?

11. Balance humidity

Ambient humidity levels are something we don't think too much about, but it's important! Whether it's in the form of winter mold or dampness in the walls during the rainy season, it can get pretty problematic. The scary part? You wouldn't even notice how it possibly makes your home smell bad since your sense of smell would get fatigued by it. But guests, however, sure will. It usually occurs in rainy or warm regions, especially in older buildings lacking appropriate ventilation.

If you've got the same problem at your home, don't worry, plants are an all-natural solution to deal with it. They're the best dehumidifiers you can get as they harvest excess moisture passively while also detoxifying the air you breathe.

12. May Improve Complexion

As unrelated as it may seem, plants can even help you achieve your skincare goals. And that's not me being a biased plant enthusiast! It comes from qualified dermatologists, who agree that by filtering out toxins from the air and balancing ambient humidity, houseplants can offer extraordinary skincare benefits.

This list of houseplant benefits isn't exhaustive by any means, but I don't want to exhaust you with them either. So... moving on.

INDOOR PLANTS ARE LOW MAINTENANCE

Aside from so many ground-breaking reasons to get house-plants, there's another big one — they're so low-maintenance. But since you're not very experienced in the realm of plant care, you can make smart moves that can further ease you into becoming a plant parent.

It's important to bear in mind that indoor gardening, just like taking on any new endeavor, is a journey that progresses with a bunch of trial and error. Depending on the weather conditions in your region and the plants you choose to bring home, these errors could be more or less. However, being observant and watching out for some well-known red flags (which you'll learn in this book later on), you can adjust your care and hopefully avoid any serious damage to your plants.

Some plants are needy and require a lot more attention than others. But, no matter how gorgeous they look, I'd suggest saving them for later — especially if you don't quite feel confident in your plant-parenting skills yet. To start, you can find so many different plants that look just as appealing without the same maintenance hassle. No, I'm not talking about those plastic ones, but real ones that genuinely thrive on low maintenance and neglect — believe it or not.

There are plants that only need to be watered once every two weeks, so if you're someone who forgets to water your plants regularly, good. Feel free to upgrade to fancier plants later on, but there's no shame in starting with one that's more your speed as a beginner.

Lady palm, zanzibar gem, snake plant (a personal favorite), asparagus, and pothos are a few examples of relatively low-maintenance plants, but there's a lot more where that came from. Succulents, for instance, have also been in trend lately and they're some of the hardest-to-kill plants you can find as long as you've got a direct-sunlight spot for them indoors.

You can also find succulents that thrive in indirect light like haworthia ones, kalanchoe, aloe, burro's tail, and gasteria. Just be sure to check on new plants regularly as variations of these species may react slightly differently in low light conditions.

TAKEAWAY

There are far too many reasons why you've got to have house-plants, and since you're reading this book, you probably feel the same way. Well, I hope your excitement has only grown after reading all those adorable fun facts about plants, and how easy some of them are to maintain. In the chapters that follow, you'll learn some priceless tips and tricks that make caring for them even simpler, maximizing your chances of becoming a successful indoor gardener in no time!

2

WATERING HACKS

A s we all learnt as kids, humans are mostly made up of water. While human adults are about 55 to 60 percent water, plants take that number and almost double it. Plants can be up to 95% water. Like us, water is a basic building block of life for them as they need it in every stage of life — from the sprouting of its seed, to its growth and sustenance.

It's a necessary element for photosynthesis — the process through which plants extract the sun's energy and produce their own food. During photosynthesis, plants extract hydrogen from the water it absorbs through roots, and also take CO_2 out of the air. In exchange, they release oxygen (which is great news for us) through their leaves' stoma, i.e. a pore.

Aside from being necessary for a plant's sustenance, water also plays another important role in regulating your plants' temperature. It helps keep them from overheating. Plants lose 90% of their water through transpiration, which is a process that accelerates in hot weather. As all the water evaporates through the stomata on its leaves, the plant can naturally absorb more water through its roots — which helps keep it cool. You can think of it as sweating but for plants!

So, if you've ever wondered how important water really is for plants — you know the answer is "pretty damn important" now. Keeping that key insight in mind, I've decided to cover all the ins and outs of watering in this paramount chapter. You'll learn watering hacks and how to manage your watering responsibilities while away — so keep reading!

HOUSEPLANT WATERING HACKS

Following our prior ruling on the importance of water for plants, it's obvious that watering is your most crucial task as a plant parent. That's sadly where many newbies make the most blunders as well. From using unsuitable water to overwatering and underwatering, there are quite a few mistakes to avoid. But don't worry, I've carefully curated this list of watering hacks to make your (and your plant's) life easier. Here we go!

1. Use Self-Watering Planters

Yep — you read that right — "self-watering" planters. They're just as good as they sound. Making smart use of mechanisms like wicking or capillary action, these planters can add water to your houseplant's soil as soon as it begins to dry out.

It saves your plants from overwatering as well because it never continuously sits in water. The soil will only draw more water in when needed, maintaining the moisture at the "just right" level at all times.

Through this simple yet life-changing tool, you can avoid a plethora of houseplant-related nightmares like root rot, yellow or brown leaves, stunted growth, and much more. Not only will your plants be healthier and happier, but you'll also have less stress as you no longer have to worry about watering.

You can find plenty of such planters online and they're not that expensive either, especially when you take their utility into account. I'd recommend finding one with a water reservoir that's transparent so you can always keep an eye on its water level. You'll have to fill it up every once in a while because the plant will slowly but surely draw water over time. The only thing you can do wrong with this setup is to forget filling up the reservoir, and having a see-through one somewhat mitigates that risk.

You could even DIY it if you're feeling adventurous. Simply type "how to build a DIY self-watering planter" into YouTube, follow along carefully, and you're golden.

2. Make Use Of Wicking

Don't wanna invest in a full-on brand-new planter? No worries, there are other ways to achieve the bliss of a self-watering system of plant care. One's wicking.

Wicking works on the same principle as the planters I've discussed above, but the mechanism isn't set up inside the pot.

It's outside, and still allows plants to water themselves as needed.

All you have to do is bury a thick cotton string or wick into the soil. Try positioning it close to the pot's center for optimal water distribution and to avoid disturbing your plant's roots. Stick the other end of the string into a water-filled container and rest it near the plant at the same level (see note below). There you have it — your self-watering system will start on its own.

The string will absorb and deliver moisture into the dry soil. As soon as the soil is saturated with its required moisture, the string stops absorbing any more of it. It'll only start when the soil demands more. Your role is to make sure the container doesn't run out of water. Fill up a large jug and you shouldn't have to worry about it for weeks! Neat, right?

Note: Ensure that the water-filled container isn't placed at a higher level than the plant pot. Making this mistake will cause gravity to keep bringing down water into the soil, which ultimately leads to overwatering, waterlogging, and eventually root rot.

3. Try Hydrospikes

New plant parents, and even some experienced ones, tend to often forget their watering duties. Similarly, some people always tend to be a bit too generous with their watering which leads to overwatering issues. If you can relate to these two categories, hydro spikes are just what you need.

They come in many designs and sizes and slowly saturate the soil with water, giving your plants the right quantity of moisture to thrive. They're positioned at the edge of the plant pot and are either connected to a container of water through a string, or have a water reservoir of their own.

Most are meant to be hidden away by big tropical plant leaves. They usually come in packs of 3 or more, with just one sufficing smaller pots and two being ideal for large pots with especially thirsty plants.

If you don't like your hydrospikes to be hidden away, you can also get ornamental ones that'll not only hydrate your houseplants, but also decorate them.

4. Burying Bottles

Just like self-watering planters, you can also make your own hydro spikes as a fun little DIY project. You'd not only be saving a few bucks, but also helping save the planet by recycling plastic bottles.

Find one with a neck that's tiny enough to hide away in the pot. Keep the lid on a screw in some holes into the plastic. You can do this carefully by pushing a heated nail or screw into it. Make some holes near the bottle's neck as well toward its top.

Fill the bottle up with water until it gets just underneath the point where the holes start. As the last step, bury the bottle neck-down into the soil. This allows water to slowly seep out of the tiny holes at the bottom. Depending on the size of the bottle, your plants should have their watering needs sorted for weeks on end.

This solution isn't ideal or preferable by any means, mainly because of refilling difficulties and how much space the bottle takes up. Still, it's a quick temporary fix that you can do just before you get ready for a flight!

5. Make Your Own Watering Can

For traditionalists who love doing it manually, a watering can is a must-have tool. Luckily, you can DIY that too and it's pretty simple! Following the same process as I've shared above, poke some holes into the lid of a plastic bottle. Fill it up with water and screw the lid on. Turn it upside down and voila — you've got your own DIY watering can. Squeeze and release the plastic bottle to regulate the pressure as you prefer.

This obviously won't win you any points for aesthetics, but it's simple, easy, and gets the job done.

6. Bottom Watering

Even as an experienced plant enthusiast, I can say that there's something about plants absorbing water for themselves, it is a concept that never gets old. That's why those time-lapses of plants doing just that are always trending on TikTok.

You can try it out with your houseplants as well. Simply place the pot into a container filled with water. The soil automatically draws up moisture through its drainage holes and the water level drops in the container over time. Once it stabilizes, you can tell that the soil needs no more water and you can remove it from the water bath. That's called bottom watering.

It's slow, sure, but it's healthier for your plants as you let it drink for itself — rather than manually pouring in more or less water than it needs through a watering can. It also leaves the top layer of the soil dry, preventing diseases and issues like fungus gnats. Plus, it lets all areas of the soil be fully saturated instead of just the sides and top, which commonly occurs with compacting.

Now here's a big caveat — you must never forget to take the plant out in time to avoid the risk of root rot. Generally, setting a timer of 20 minutes or so should do the trick, but it slightly varies with the size of the pot you're working with.

7. Bleach

If you're into propagating (which we'll get into later on in this book), this one's for you. Successfully propagating houseplants isn't a piece of cake. You have to change the water frequently — and that part can easily slip out of your mind. Failure to do so can lead to bacterial growth and lack of oxygenation for the roots. If you only remember to change water once it's murky, it's probably already too late. It may mean damaged roots, stunted new growth, and overall — a failed propagation attempt.

Here's your saving grace: bleach. Adding only a few drops of it gives you some more leeway as it prevents bacterial growth for a few more days. By keeping your vase water healthier for longer, your cut flowers have an extended lifeline in case you forget to change the water.

But be careful not to add too much bleach! It can change the water's pH level which limits the uptake in your plant cuttings. All you need is just a couple of drops and you're set.

8. Leave Your Water Out

Not many people know this, but tap water isn't necessarily good for your plants. That's because not all tap water is the same. In most locations, the town's water supply adds certain chemicals in it to make it safe for drinking. One example is chlorine, the exposure to which isn't ideal for plants.

That's why experienced gardeners only use distilled, filtered, or rainwater for their houseplants. Sure, using tap water once in a while won't hurt, but regular use leads to chlorine buildup which can severely damage houseplants.

If using filtered, distilled, or rainwater is too much of a hassle, simply try leaving some water out before using it. This allows excess chlorine to evaporate away, making the water healthier for your sensitive plants.

For best results, leave the water out for at least 24 to 48 hours.

9. Putting Your Plants in the Shower Helps Remove Dust and Pests

In their natural habitat, most plants get showered down by rainfall occasionally. That's a privilege that indoor houseplants miss out on, but you could replicate some of the effects by putting them under your shower in the bathroom. Just a few minutes is good enough to rinse the leaves from top to bottom, drenching the soil until water starts to freely flow out of the drainage holes at the bottom. This hydrates, nourishes, and washes your plants, along with many other benefits!

10. Tropical plants love the extra moisture

Aside from all the benefits mentioned above, you get bonus points if you have tropical plant species because they love the extra bit of moisture and humidity in the shower. Examples of such plants include Philodendrons, Rhaphidophora, Alocasias and Monsteras. Leave these plants under your shower from time to time to stimulate the natural refreshing rain they'd get out in the open. Just a few minutes should do the trick!

11. Showering help reduce excess salt buildup

We've discussed the threat of chlorine buildup in the plants above, and it's the same case with salt. With container house-plants, minerals don't get widely distributed since there's not much soil around. As a result, excess salts that commonly come from fertilizers will linger and slowly build up. They're visible in the form of crusty white deposits around the drainage holes and at the soil line around the pot. The heavier the buildup, the greater the risk of issues like reduced growth, brown leaves, wilting, and lower leaves dropping. All of this occurs because the salt gets in the way of the plant's water absorption. To avoid it, try giving your plants a good wash every season!

HOW TO WASH QUICKLY AND EASILY

Let's start with the easiest way of them all — leaving your houseplants out in the rain. Doing so once every season should save you all the trouble of manually rinsing your plants.

But unfortunately, not every region in the world gets regular rainfall, so here's an easy way to do the job by yourself.

First, gently remove any loose debris or dead leaves from your plant. Then, take your plant to the shower or outside to a shady area.

Using lukewarm water, gently rinse your plant, making sure to wet both the leaves and the soil. Be sure to use a gentle stream of water, as too much force can damage delicate foliage. If your plant has a lot of dust or grime on its leaves, you can use a soft cloth or sponge to wipe each leaf.

If you notice any pests on your plant, such as spider mites or scale insects, you can use a mixture of mild dish soap and water to wash them off. Mix one teaspoon of dish soap with one quart of water and apply the solution to the plant with a spray bottle, making sure to cover both the leaves and the soil. Rinse the plant thoroughly with water after a few minutes.

Make sure you let your plant dry completely before returning it to its pot or original location. You can use a towel to gently pat down the leaves, but be careful not to rub them too hard, as this can cause damage.

One additional tip is to consider using a handheld showerhead or a watering wand with a shower setting for washing your plants. This can help you control the water flow and avoid accidentally breaking off delicate leaves.

Remember, every plant has its own care requirements, so be sure to check the care instructions for your specific plant before washing it.

With these simple tips, your houseplants will be looking fresh and clean in no time!

PLANT SITTERS

Just like pets, houseplants are living things — and since they're not in their natural habitats, they rely on regular care from you to survive and thrive. But that doesn't mean you have to kiss holidays goodbye for good! If the watering hacks aren't enough to keep your plants healthy while you're away, there's always another route you can take — and that's hiring a plant sitter!

A plant sitter can take care of your plant's watering, trimming, pruning, and even repotting needs for a certain period while you're away for a holiday. You can also book one-time visits for your houseplants' upkeep or simply making sure they're okay. You can either give them access to your garden while you're away, or leave your houseplants with them for "plant-sitting" until you're back.

When Do You Need Them?

Plant sitting services can come in handy if you're going to be away for more than a few days, especially if you have sensitive or delicate plants that require regular attention. Plants can dry out quickly without water, and too much water can also be harmful. A plant sitter can make sure your plants are getting the right amount of water and can also keep an eye out for any signs of trouble, such as yellowing leaves or pest infestations.

Having a plant sitter can give you peace of mind while you're away and ensure that your plants stay healthy and happy. Just be sure to give your plant sitter clear instructions on how to care for your plants, including watering schedules, plant food requirements, and any other special needs your plants may have.

Tips for Finding a Quality Sitter

- **Ask around.**

Reach out to friends, family, and neighbors to see if they know anyone who might be interested in plant sitting. You might be surprised at who in your community has a green thumb!

- **Look online.**

Check online Websites like Rover or Care.com can help you find local pet and plant sitters in your area. You can also look on social media platforms like Facebook or Nextdoor for local plant care groups or ask for recommendations from gardening groups.

- **Look for experience.**

When interviewing potential plant sitters, ask about their experience caring for plants. Have they cared for a wide variety of plants? Do they know how to recognize and treat common plant problems? Make sure they have the experience needed to care for your specific plants.

- **Communication is key.**

Find someone who is willing to communicate with you regularly. They should be able to update you on how your plants are doing and ask for advice if they encounter any problems.

- **Trust your gut.**

Ultimately, you want to find someone you feel comfortable leaving your plants with. If something doesn't feel right, keep looking until you find a sitter that you feel confident in.

FINAL TAKEAWAY

In this chapter, you've learned about the supreme importance of watering for houseplants, as well as various creative ways and hacks for getting it right. With all this knowledge added to your plant-parenting arsenal, you'll hopefully have a much higher success rate by avoiding silly blunders. After all, most houseplant deaths are associated with watering mistakes, and that's extremely unfortunate considering how easy it is to get it right as seen in this chapter.

Even while you're away, your plants can take care of their own watering needs through simple tools like a wicking mechanism or a self-watering planter. These are either super cheap to buy or very easy to make on a DIY basis. As an additional precautionary measure, you can also hire a plant sitter to take over your parenting responsibilities temporarily until you're back as that's the safest route out there!

In the next chapter, we're looking at some of my favorite hacks for your desk plants!

3

HACKS FOR DESK PLANTS

As we've brushed upon in earlier chapters, enriching your workspace with a touch of greenery has a plethora of benefits. It helps you manage stress, be more creative, and therefore more productive! It all stems from an innate human desire that we all have which is to connect with nature — which is called 'biophilia'. Sadly, though, most people fail to take advantage of this concept and continue to spend a big chunk of their day in boring, stuffy workspaces devoid of any element of nature.

With more and more of us working from home in 2023, there's no reason not to have some houseplants on your desk. They allow you to breathe cleaner, fresher air during your deep focus sessions. They even help you keep your stress levels in check. And that's not just my personal experience with houseplants (that too, though) — it's backed by science.

According to a study conducted in 2010 by the University of Technology in Sydney, the introduction of plants in the workplace resulted in considerable reduction in stress levels among employees. The study reported anxiety and tension lowered by 37%, a 58% decline in feelings of dejection or depression, a 44% drop in hostility and anger, and a 38% drop in fatigue.

That's groundbreaking, and it's exactly why more and more offices are incorporating more plants into their interior decor as an effortless way to see a significant boost in staff spirits.

That's why I've dedicated this chapter completely to desk plants. Here, you'll find my recommendations for the best desk plants, along with tips for keeping them alive and thriving in an office environment or your work-from-home setup. I'll also share some fun and creative DIY projects to personalize your desk plant display. By the end of this chapter, you'll have all the knowledge you need to create your own perfect desk plant oasis.

BEST DESK PLANTS

For this selection of desk plants, I've prioritized species that have a whole bunch of workplace-related benefits without being too needy when it comes to maintenance. After all, we're looking to bring your stress levels down, not the other way around! Let's begin.

1. Devil's Ivy

Devil's Ivy is commonly called Pothos (even though they're not the same, but let's not get technical), and it'll make for a wonderful addition to your work desk. It's an evergreen vine having lovely, heart-shaped leaves that are large and vibrant. The plant is highly adaptive and can adjust to different types of indoor conditions, no matter if it's a dark or a well-lit office space. Definitely a #1 pick if you'd ask me.

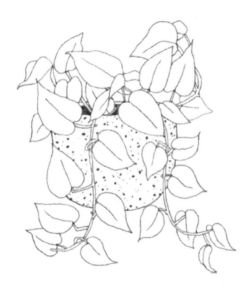

2. Aglaonema

We all know houseplants to be green, but some are unique. That's what sets this plant apart. Its leaves tend to have gorgeous traces of silver and red color which can add tons of aesthetic value to your workspace. You can add a vibrant pop to your otherwise sober-looking desk setup!

3. Ficus Benjamina

The Ficus Benjamina, better known as the weeping fig, is another top contender in my list of desk plant recommendations. This plant is versatile enough to look great on its own or when it shares the stage with a mixed selection.

It grows wild in Southeast Asian forests as well as Northern Australia. They're not very high-maintenance, but keep in mind that direct cold drafts from doors, windows, or air conditioners can be harmful to the plant. So, try to place it in a spot where these drafts won't reach the plant directly.

4. Zamioculcas Zamiifolia

Next, we have the ZZ plant. The full name is pretty hard to pronounce, but the plant itself is just as easy to maintain. It has bulging roots and thick stalks that can retain large amounts of water. This means you won't have to water the plant too frequently which takes off a big chunk of pressure as a plant parent!

The ZZ plant can also live for long periods despite only being exposed to low light. It also naturally doesn't suffer from pest problems as often and doesn't need much fertilizer to thrive. It makes total sense that this hassle-free plant is a favorite among plant parents who are guilty of killing their houseplants!

5. Bromeliads

If you'd ask me, the Bromeliad is one of the coolest-looking plants that you can add to your interior decor. Making it bloom may not be the easiest task, but once it does, the plant won't need much effort from you in the way of care and maintenance. Just some occasional watering and they'll thrive! They don't even need much fertilizer either, so I'd highly recommend this one for its gorgeous blooms and striking colors.

6. Philodendron

Philodendrons were discovered in the 1800s, and have since been a popular pick among houseplant enthusiasts. It's a man-made hybrid with big, glossy, deep-green leaves. The large leaves look stunning in an indoor setting and maintain their luscious appearance in the shade as well.

The plant naturally thrives in temperatures within the range of 65 to 68 degrees Fahrenheit. It's the perfect choice if you plan on placing it in the corner as part of a large display alongside Imperial Greens or other unique-looking plant species to bring a tinge of mother nature into your office decor.

7. Peace Lily

Here's another common houseplant species that makes for an excellent addition to your workspace. The Peace Lily has broad, wide, dark green leaves and grows the prettiest white flowers in bloom. That's in fact where the name "Lily" comes from.

They're ideal for newbie plant parents as they're fairly forgiving of overwatering mistakes, and don't need much light to thrive either!

Aside from its aesthetic value, the peace lily plant is also a great cleaning agent for the air inside your office or workspace. It removes toxins and provides a nice environment for you to work in!

8. Dracaena

If you're looking for a desk plant that's especially tough to kill, you can't go wrong with Dracaenas. Not only are they highly resilient, but also do a tremendous job of getting rid of pollutants in your air. Calling this plant "easy to care for" would be an understatement because it can literally even survive in drought-like conditions. It naturally has a beastly root system that makes wilting very unlikely. This makes it capable of forgiving a fair amount of negligence on your part — but that's not your license to be careless!

9. Sansevieria

Funnily called the "mother-in-law's tongue" — Sansevieria has long pointy leaves, with the nickname referring to the sharp tongue of the stereotypical mother-in-law! It's also called the snake plant, so make of that what you will.

Nevertheless, the sinister-looking aesthetic of a plant makes for a great visual stimulus inside the office. It's also highly survivable and can go without water for up to a month, even in low light. It can also withstand lengthened sun exposure. But those aren't the ideal conditions for your snake plant to thrive, so be sure to give it adequate care and maintenance.

10. Cacti

If you know yourself to be especially negligent and forgetful when it comes to looking after your plants, a cactus could be your best friend. That's because they're arguably the only type of plants that not only don't mind negligence, but actually thrive on it. Since cacti naturally retain such a high amount of water within them, they tend to be just fine without being watered for weeks. But they do need more light or sun than other plants, so getting one may only be a good idea if your desk gets enough natural light during the day.

11. Peperomia Ginny

If you have a tight and cozy office space and don't get enough light in it, don't worry, there are plants that can thrive in those conditions as well. Take for example, the Peperomia Ginny. It's a slow-growing species that can only be found in sub-par lighting. But when possible, occasionally move this plant to a spot with medium to bright light.

12. Modern Bamboo

Here's a personal favorite — Modern Bamboo! Aside from its intriguing, special, and catchy appearance, it's also considered as a symbol of good fortune and luck. I could personally use a lot of that in my workspace.

I love how little effort this guy takes. Just place it somewhere with a moderate amount of indirect daylight, and give it some water when the top layer of the soil feels dry to your touch. That's it!

13. Monstera

If you've got some floor space to spare in your office and want a plant that doubles as a statement piece in your interior decor, go for the Monstera! Because of how the leaves look, it is also sometimes called the Swiss Cheese plant. Finding a good spot for it mainly comes down to your personal preference because this guy grows well almost anywhere requiring very little light. Remember to feed it monthly with some plant food and water it when the soil's top half dries out.

TIPS TO KEEP DESK PLANTS ALIVE

We already know the groundbreaking benefits that plants have to offer in your workspace. But in return, you've got to give your green friend the care and love it deserves. In boring terms, it's called necessary maintenance. Now how much of it is required depends on the type of plant you've chosen. Different species have contrasting needs in terms of lighting, watering, humidity levels, or even pruning.

Here's a list of hacks to make your maintenance duties as easy as possible!

1. Expose to more lighting

Let's start with lighting. Every plant needs light to sustain itself since it's necessary for carrying out photosynthesis. But not all species need it to the same extent. Almost all indoor plants, for instance, require very little light to thrive which allows them to be domesticated safely. They mostly come from low-light origins in nature, occupying spots like rainforest floors where direct sunlight barely reaches. This makes indoor settings not only livable for them, but more suitable in some cases.

Make sure you're exposing your plants to some level of direct or indirect lighting as per the needs of their particular species.

Occasionally spin the pot to make sure the plant gets even lighting on all sides. If your plant still displays symptoms of low light exposure (such as lighter foliage or lankiness), try placing some artificial sunlight bulbs to make up for the lack of natural lighting.

As a beginner, it's wise to stick to relatively resilient plants that are super hard to kill even if you fail to offer them optimal lighting conditions. Examples include snake plants, philodendrons, android palms.

2. Water Your Plants Regularly

Water is another key component in photosynthesis, and plants can't survive without it. But ironically, it's also one of the leading causes of houseplant deaths around the world. Too little or too much of it can both be fatal to your plant.

Set reminders to avoid forgetting waterings and try maintaining a consistent schedule. But never overwater your plants! Always check if the soil is still damp from your last watering, and if so, the plant doesn't need any more water. Wait for at least the top layer of the soil to completely dry out before watering.

Look out for brown tips on your plant's leaves as that's an indication of underwatering. Signs of overwatering, on the other hand, are fungus gnats and yellowing leaves. So if you've already noticed any of these red flags, adjust your watering habits accordingly.

3. Up the humidity

A common reason for tropical plants to struggle in indoor settings is drier climates in offices. You can make up for this by investing in a humidifier or vaporizer for your workspace. These can absorb moist air from the environment and point it in the direction of your display of plants. This way, your plants will have enhanced protection against pests and diseases.

4. Trimming

When it comes to indoor plants, aesthetics do matter since they add to your overall interior decor. That's why it's important to keep your plants looking neat and tidy all the time, which is only achievable through timely pruning and trimming. This includes getting rid of withered limbs, unwanted leaves, over-growth, and dried herbs. A set of cutters and plant snippers should do the trick. To encourage fresh growth, carefully trim the ends of dominating branches and stems in the pot. You'll find more tips at the end of this list!

5. Find the Right Pot

You'd think choosing a pot isn't a significant decision from a plant care standpoint — you'd be wrong. Most people prefer pots with a fancy design or ones that match the room well, but those should be the last of your concerns when choosing a pot for your houseplants. Size, for instance, matters most — and plays a pivotal role in determining your plants' growth and health. An oversized one can potentially lead to root rot, whereas a pot that's too small can quickly dry out the soil.

Aside from the size being just right, also consider the pot's material. In plastic ones, soil tends to retain its moisture for longer, giving you more downtime before the plant needs another watering. But, depending on the plant you're working with, that's not always a good thing. Some plants thrive in drier soil, in which case Terra-cotta pots would be your best friends.

6. Choose Plants That Are Easy To Care For

As a beginner, you've got to pace yourself. There's no shame in choosing houseplants that are easy to care for. In fact, that's possibly the most effective move you can make to prevent the guilt of killing a plant. Plants like cacti, succulents, geraniums, sago palms, and areca palms are simple to care for and don't ask for much maintenance. Once you find success looking after them and taking care of their limited needs, feel free to move on to more challenging projects.

For the same reason, you can never go wrong with peace lilies and ZZ plants as your first few adoptions. Once you experience the benefits it has on your productivity, mental health, and efficiency, feel free to expand your collection of office plants to reap even more benefits.

7. Pruning Tips

Not all plants require frequent pruning, but some vining species do. You'll learn that quite quickly if you're a Pothos owner like me!

It's like giving your plants a haircut, though not nearly as technical. Still, here are a few tips to bear in mind to help ensure a job well done.

- **Timing is key**

Prune your plants during the appropriate season for optimal growth. Different plants have different pruning requirements, so make sure to research and understand the right time to prune each type of plant in your garden.

- **Use the right tools**

Invest in good quality pruning tools such as sharp pruning shears, loppers, and saws that are appropriate for the size and type of branches you are pruning. Clean and sanitize your tools before each use to prevent the spread of diseases.

- **Follow the 3 Ds**

When pruning, focus on the 3 Ds - Dead, Diseased, and Damaged branches. Remove any dead, diseased, or damaged branches to promote healthy growth and prevent the spread of diseases to other parts of the plant.

- **Don't over-prune**

Avoid over-pruning, as it can weaken the plant and reduce its ability to produce flowers or fruits. Always aim to maintain the natural shape and structure of the plant while removing only what is necessary.

- **Prune to another growing point**

When making pruning cuts, avoid leaving stubs with no growing point. Instead, prune to a healthy bud, node, or lateral branch that is facing outward to encourage new growth in the desired direction.

- **Pay attention to pruning cuts**

Make clean and precise pruning cuts at a 45-degree angle just above a node or bud. Avoid leaving stubs or making ragged cuts, as they can provide entry points for diseases and pests.

Pruning is an art that takes practice, so don't be afraid to experiment and try different methods to see what works best for your plants. Gardening centers are a great resource, where friendly experts can provide valuable suggestions and guidance on pruning techniques tailored to your specific plants. Remember, with patience and practice, you'll become a pruning pro and your garden will thrive!

Desk Plants DIY for Aesthetics

- **DIY Wall-Mounted Plant Shelf**

Create a stylish and space-saving plant display by making a wall-mounted plant shelf using wooden planks and brackets. Perfect for adding a touch of greenery to your home office without taking up valuable desk space!"

- **DIY Terrarium**

Build your own terrarium using a glass container, succulents, and decorative pebbles for a low-maintenance and visually stunning addition to your home office desk. A mini green oasis that brings nature right to your fingertips!

- **DIY Hanging Planters**

Get crafty and make your own hanging planters using macrame, rope, or even repurposed containers. Hang them above your desk to create a vertical garden that adds a pop of color and life to your workspace!

- **DIY Potted Plants**

Personalize your home office desk with DIY potted plants by repotting your favorite plants into stylish containers such as mason jars, painted pots, or vintage cups. A budget-friendly way to add a touch of charm and personality to your workspace!

- **DIY Plant Stand**

Create a custom plant stand using wood, metal, or even repurposed furniture to elevate your plants and create a focal point in your home office. A functional and decorative way to showcase your beloved plant collection!

- **DIY Plant Wall**

Make a statement with a DIY plant wall using shelves, hooks, or even repurposed pallets to create a stunning vertical garden backdrop for your home office. A bold and eye-catching way to bring the beauty of nature indoors!

- **DIY Plant Hangers**

Add a boho vibe to your home office with DIY plant hangers made from rope, macrame, or even old t-shirts. Hang them from the ceiling or on the walls to create a whimsical and eco-friendly plant display!

- **DIY Desk Garden**

Create a mini garden on your home office desk using small planters, trays, or even repurposed drawers. A delightful and functional way to have a mini ecosystem at your fingertips, promoting relaxation and productivity!

- **DIY Plant Arrangements**

Get creative with DIY plant arrangements by combining different types of plants, textures, and colors in unique containers such as terracotta pots, tea cups, or vintage tins. A fun and artistic way to express your green thumb and add visual interest to your workspace!

- **DIY Plant Art**

Make your own plant art by framing pressed flowers, leaves, or even botanical prints to add a touch of nature-inspired decor to your home office. A personalized and meaningful way to infuse your workspace with the beauty of the natural world!

FINAL TAKEAWAY

So to wrap things up, caring for desk plants is not just about adding a touch of green to your workspace, but also about creating a thriving ecosystem that boosts your mood and productivity. By following these tips, from finding the perfect spot for your plant to providing the right amount of water, light, and nutrients, you can ensure your desk plant flourishes and becomes a source of inspiration. Remember to keep an eye out for signs of distress and adjust your care accordingly. So go ahead, give your desk plant the TLC (tender loving care) it deserves, and watch it thrive, bringing joy and vitality to your workday! Happy gardening!

Well, buckle up, because in the next chapter, "Propagation Methods for Houseplants," you're about to discover the thrilling world of plant propagation. From the exhilarating thrill of taking a simple cutting and watching it root and grow into a flourishing plant, to the ingenious hacks that will turbocharge your propagation success, this chapter will unlock the secrets to multiplying your houseplant collection like a horticultural wizard.

4

PROPAGATION METHODS FOR HOUSEPLANTS

P ropagation is the process of initiating new plants out of your existing ones. But, if you do it wrong, you can sadly end up harming or even killing them, which is why it's crucial to learn how to do it right. With the information and tips shared in this all-important chapter, you'll avoid some common propagating mistakes and master the correct method of propagation to produce healthy new plants and multiply your collection!

Here's everything we'll be going over:

- **Cuttings:** Learn how to take cuttings from stems or leaves of houseplants and root them to create new plants.
- **By Division:** Discover how to divide mature houseplants into smaller sections, each with its own root system, to propagate them.

- **Offsets and Plantlets:** Explore how certain houseplants produce offsets or plantlets, which can be separated from the parent plant and used for propagation.
- **Air Layering:** Find out about the technique of air layering, where a stem of a houseplant is partially cut and encouraged to form roots before being detached from the parent plant.
- **Seed Sowing:** Learn about the process of sowing seeds of houseplants and how to care for them to successfully grow new plants.
- **More Tips and Tricks:** Get additional tips and tricks for successful houseplant propagation, including timing, equipment, and care for newly propagated plants.

These sections provide an overview of the different methods that will be covered in the chapter, giving you a glimpse into the range of techniques you can use to propagate their houseplants. So without further ado, let's jump in.

PROPAGATING CUTTINGS

Let's start with one of the most common ways of propagation used for houseplants — through cuttings. We'll look at three examples of suitable plants for propagating cuttings and how exactly you should go about it.

1. African Violet

The simplest way to propagate an African violet is to break off a leaf off the main stem while leaving its leaf stem (also called people) attached. Place the petiole into some moist potting mix or just water. As soon as roots begin to form, pot up the leaves that have been submerged in the water — simple as that!

2. Begonia

Another easy plant to propagate through leaf cuttings is Begonia. Simply extract a healthy leaf from your plant and lay it down on top of some moist potting mix. Slice a few of its veins through using a clean knife and gently pin down the leaf into the soil using toothpicks. The goal is to bring the potting mix in contact with the cuts in your leaf.

Keep the soil moist and use a plastic wrap or bag to cover the pot, creating a make-do greenhouse of sorts. Plantlets should grow from the cuts and you can start potting them once they grow a couple leaves of their own.

3. Snake Plant

Last but not the least, we have the snake plant. Not only is it easy to care for (as we've learned in earlier chapters), but also to propagate! Simply cut one of its leaves into smaller parts using some sterile pruning shears. Create angular incisions aiming to bring its bottom ends toward a center point. Dip those ends in rooting powder and tuck them into moist potting soil. Soon, some brand new snake plant babies should start to form on the sides of those leaf sections.

The Various Cuttings Methods

With those examples out of the way, let's now look at the various ways in which you can snip your parent plants for propagation. There's no "best" one as they all shine in different scenarios depending on the plant you're propagating and several other factors.

1. Stem Cutting

This is one of the most common methods of propagation. It involves taking a section of the stem from a healthy parent plant and encouraging it to root and grow into a new plant. Here's how you can do it:

- Select a healthy stem that has several leaves and nodes (the points where leaves are attached to the stem).
- Using a sharp and clean pair of scissors or pruning shears, make a clean cut just below a node.
- Remove any lower leaves from the stem, leaving a few leaves at the top.
- Dip the cut end of the stem in a rooting hormone (optional, but it can help promote root growth).
- Plant the stem cutting in a well-draining potting mix or a rooting medium, and keep it moist but not waterlogged.
- Place the cutting in a warm, bright spot with indirect light, and mist the leaves regularly to maintain humidity.

In a few weeks to a few months, you should see new roots and shoots emerging from the cutting, indicating that it has successfully rooted.

2. Leaf Cutting

This method is commonly used for plants with thick, fleshy leaves, such as succulents and certain types of begonias as covered in one of the examples above. Here are some easy to follow steps for it:

- Gently remove a healthy leaf from the parent plant, making sure to include the entire leaf, including the base or petiole.
- Allow the leaf to dry and callus for a day or two to prevent rotting.
- Place the leaf on top of a well-draining potting mix or a succulent/cactus mix, with the petiole end inserted slightly into the soil.
- Mist the leaf and keep the soil slightly moist, but be careful not to overwater.
- Place the pot in a warm, bright spot with indirect light, and avoid direct sunlight.

Within a month or so, you'll hopefully find new roots and a tiny plantlet emerging from the base of the leaf, which can eventually be potted up into a new plant.

3. Leaf with Petiole

This method is similar to leaf cutting, but it involves taking a leaf with a longer stem called a petiole — similar to our African Violet example. Here's how you can do it:

- Gently remove a healthy leaf from the parent plant, including the petiole.
- Place the petiole in water, making sure that only the petiole is submerged and the leaf is kept above water.

- Change the water regularly to prevent stagnation and rot.
- Once roots have formed on the petiole, carefully plant it in a well-draining potting mix, burying the roots but keeping the leaf above the soil.
- Keep the soil slightly moist and place the pot in a warm, bright spot with indirect light.

New growth should eventually emerge from the base of the leaf, indicating that the plantlet has established itself.

4. Leaf Sections

This method is commonly used for plants with large leaves that can be divided into smaller sections. Follow these steps to try it out if you're planning to propagate something like a snake plant:

- Gently remove a healthy leaf from the parent plant.
- Cut the leaf into smaller sections, making sure that each section has at least one vein or a portion of the leaf stem (midrib).
- Dip the cut ends of the leaf sections in a rooting hormone (optional).
- Plant the leaf sections in a well-draining potting mix, burying the cut ends and keeping the leaf sections upright.
- Mist the leaf sections and keep the soil slightly moist.
- Place the pot in a warm, bright spot with indirect light.

Depending on what you're propagating, you should see new growth emerging from the base of your leaf sections which tells you they've rooted and have started to develop into new plants.

5. Root Cuttings

If your plant has thick roots — enough to be able to cut up into smaller sections — this method of propagating through cuttings can be promising! Follow these steps:

- Carefully dig up a healthy parent plant and locate a healthy, fleshy root.
- Using clean pruning shears or a sharp knife, cut a section of the root, making sure it has at least one growth bud.
- Plant the root cutting in a well-draining potting mix with the cut end facing downwards.
- Keep the soil slightly moist, but avoid overwatering.
- Place the pot in a warm, bright spot with indirect light.

With time, you should see new shoots emerging from the top of the root cutting!

Remember to always use clean and sharp tools when taking cuttings, and be sure to use a well-draining potting mix or rooting medium to prevent root rot. It's also important to keep the cuttings in a warm, bright spot with indirect light and maintain appropriate moisture levels to promote successful rooting.

Pro Tips To Become a PROpagator!

Ready to take on the thrill of propagating houseplants from cuttings? Get ready to become a plant parent extraordinaire with these essential tips!

- **Start with a Healthy Mother Plant**

The health of the mother plant is crucial to the success of your cuttings. Choose a mature, healthy plant with no signs of disease or pest infestation. Avoid taking cuttings from weak or stressed plants, as they may not root well and could produce weak offspring.

- **Use a Soilless Mix**

When propagating cuttings, I'd suggest using a well-draining soilless mix, such as a combination of perlite and peat moss or vermiculite and coconut coir. Soilless mixes provide good aeration and moisture retention, which are essential for root development.

- **Rooting Powder is a Great Aid**

Rooting powder or rooting hormone can be a helpful tool in promoting root development. It contains hormones that stimulate root growth and can increase the success rate of rooting, especially for harder-to-root plants. Simply dip the cut end of the cutting into the rooting powder before planting it in the rooting medium.

- **Provide Bright Light but Avoid Direct Sunlight**

Newly propagated cuttings need bright light to promote healthy growth, but direct sunlight can be too intense and may cause stress or damage to the delicate new roots. Place your cuttings in a location with bright, indirect light, such as near a window with filtered sunlight or under artificial grow lights.

- **Keep Evenly Moist Throughout the Process**

Maintaining consistent moisture levels can help boost your chances of successful rooting. Keep the rooting medium evenly moist, but not soaking wet, throughout the propagation process. Avoid allowing the cuttings to dry out completely or sitting in standing water, as both can hinder root development.

- **Keep an Eye on Humidity**

Humidity is also a critical factor in propagating cuttings, as it helps prevent excessive moisture loss through the leaves and promotes root development. You can increase humidity around the cuttings by covering them with a plastic bag, using a humidity dome, or placing them in a propagator. Be sure to check for condensation and provide ventilation to prevent mold or mildew growth.

- **Transfer to Potting Soil When Roots Have Developed**

Here comes the best part! Once the cuttings have developed roots, it's time to transfer them to pots with normal potting soil. It's an exciting milestone in your propagation journey and as someone who's been doing it for years, I can tell you it never really gets old.

Once you see those roots starting to develop, it's time to give your baby plants their own space to grow. Gently transfer them to pots filled with normal potting soil, taking care not to damage the delicate roots. For easy-to-grow plants, this can happen in just a few days, while for more stubborn ones, it may take several months. Remember to water them regularly and provide them with the right amount of light, and watch your cuttings thrive and grow into healthy, happy plants in their new pots. It's like watching your little ones leave the nest and spread their roots in their new homes!

- **Be Patient**

Propagating cuttings can be a rewarding process, but it requires patience. Rooting can take time, and not all cuttings will be successful. It's important to be patient and allow the natural process of root development to occur at its own pace. Don't be discouraged by failures and keep experimenting with different plants and methods to find what works best for you.

Remember to provide proper care and attention to your cuttings during the propagation process, and don't hesitate to experiment and learn from your experiences. With time, practice, and patience, you can become proficient in propagating houseplants from cuttings and enjoy the satisfaction (and not to mention, cost-savings) of growing new plants of your own!

PROPAGATE BY DIVISION

Looking for an efficient way to multiply your houseplants and expand your indoor jungle? Propagation by division might just be the answer. This simple and effective method involves dividing a mature plant into multiple smaller plants, each with its own roots and shoots.

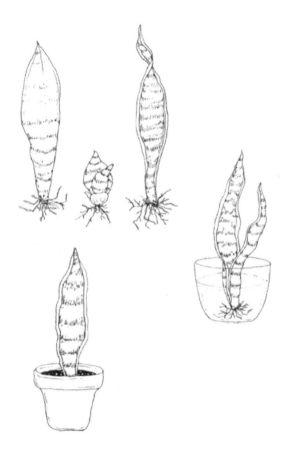

It's particularly useful for houseplants that naturally produce many offshoots or pups from their roots, such as Aspidistra, Boston Fern, and Calathea. With just a little know-how, you can easily propagate and multiply your plant collection, filling your home with even more lush greenery.

Examples of Suitable Houseplants

Aspidistra

Aspidistra plants produce multiple offshoots or pups from the base of the plant, making them ideal candidates for propagation by division. These offshoots already have their own set of roots attached, which increases their chances of successful propagation.

Boston Fern

Boston Ferns have a clumping growth habit with a dense root ball, which makes them well-suited for propagation by division. Dividing the root ball into smaller sections with healthy fronds allows each section to establish itself as an individual plant with its own roots and foliage. This method is a great way to rejuvenate an overgrown Boston Fern or create new plants to expand your collection or share with others.

Calathea

Calathea plants often produce multiple stems with leaves from a central root ball, so it makes sense why the plant is usually propagated by division. If everything goes well, each divided section develops into a new Calathea plant with its unique foliage patterns. This method helps to maintain the overall health and appearance of the parent plant while also allowing you to propagate and enjoy more Calathea plants in different areas of your home!

Steps to Create Divisions

If you've got a plant that naturally produces many pups or offshoots, propagating by division makes the most sense for multiplying your plant family! Follow these simple steps to create your divisions:

- **Step 1** Carefully remove the whole plant from its pot, taking care not to damage the roots or foliage. Gently pull each pup away from the main root ball. To tackle stubborn roots, you can use a soil knife or a trowel to slice through them. The goal is to try and retain as many roots as you can with every individual pup.
- **Step 2** Once you've separated the pups, immediately transfer them into new containers as soon as possible. Plant each division into its own pot filled with well-draining potting mix, making sure to bury the roots and leave the foliage above the soil surface.
- **Step 3** Maintain an even level of moisture in the soil for several weeks to encourage those disturbed roots to start growing again.
- **Step 4** Keep your plants out of direct sunlight. After about 10 days, you can start moving them into a spot with brighter light. To boost healthy growth, give them some houseplant fertilizer at ½ strength.

Tips

Here are 5 helpful tips for propagating plants by division:

- **Choose healthy and mature plants**

When propagating by division, it's important to select plants that are healthy, mature, and well-established. These plants are more likely to have developed sufficient root systems and foliage to successfully propagate through division.

- **Use clean and sharp tools**

Make sure to use clean and sharp scissors, pruning shears, or a clean knife when creating divisions. This helps to minimize the risk of spreading diseases or damaging the plant during the division process.

- **Dividing at the right time**

Timing is crucial when it comes to division. Propagate plants by division during their active growing season, when they are actively producing new growth and have sufficient energy reserves to support the divided sections.

- **Properly prepare the divisions**

Ensure that each divided section has enough roots and foliage to establish itself as an independent plant. Trim back any damaged or diseased foliage and remove any excess soil from the root ball to expose the individual offshoots or pups.

- **Provide appropriate care after division**

Once the divisions are potted, provide them with proper care, including appropriate light, humidity, and watering. Keep the soil evenly moist and avoid overwatering or underwatering. Monitor the progress of the divisions closely and make adjustments to the care routine as needed.

Division Troubleshooting Tips

If you're new to propagating (or even if it's not your first rodeo), things might not always go according to plan. Despite your best efforts to do things just right, some tricky factors like the environment or some natural human error can lead to issues. Don't worry though, this section helps you troubleshoot exactly what might have gone wrong. I'll go over the four most common scenarios that take place whenever there's a complication in the process of propagation by division — as well as what you need to do in each case for prevention and damage control.

Scenario #1 Divided Plants Survive but Fail to Thrive:

- Make sure you plant the divided plants in soil that meets their specific needs, including good drainage, proper pH levels, and adequate nutrients.

- Be mindful of your watering habits and avoid overwatering or underwatering the divided plants, as it can lead to root rot or dehydration.
- Provide plenty of sunlight based on the sunlight requirements of the divided plants. Too much or too little sunlight can affect their growth and health.
- Give the divided plants enough space to grow without overcrowding them, as competition for resources can hinder their growth.

Scenario #2 Divided Plants Don't Survive After Replanting:

- Handle the divided plants with care during the division process to minimize damage to their roots and other plant parts.
- Plant the divided plants as soon as possible after dividing them, or keep the roots moist and protected if replanting is delayed.
- Plant the divided plants at the right depth, avoiding planting them too deep or too shallow, as it can affect their ability to establish roots and grow.
- Consider using a rooting hormone to encourage root development and increase their chances of survival.

Scenario #3 Divided Plants Growing Well but Not Flowering:

- Check if the divided plants are getting enough sunlight for their specific flowering requirements. Some plants need a certain amount of sunlight to initiate flowering.

- Ensure that the divided plants are receiving adequate nutrients, including phosphorus, which is important for flower development. You can use a balanced fertilizer or add compost or organic matter to improve soil fertility.
- Avoid over-fertilizing the divided plants, as excessive nitrogen can promote vegetative growth at the expense of flowering.
- Remember that some plants may take a few seasons to establish themselves and start flowering, so be patient!

Scenario #4 Established Plants Declining in Vigor:

- Check for signs of pests or diseases on the established plants, as infestations or infections can weaken the plants. Take appropriate measures to control pests or diseases if detected.
- Ensure that the established plants are planted in soil with proper drainage and nutrient levels.
- Consider dividing the established plants again if they have become overcrowded, as overcrowding can lead to competition for resources and result in declining vigor.
- Regularly prune the established plants to remove dead or diseased parts, promote airflow, and stimulate new growth.

Remember to research and understand the specific needs of the plants you are propagating by division, and don't hesitate to observe, care for, and intervene as needed.

Let's Look at an Example — Peace Lily

Having covered propagating by division in depth, let's now look at a pretty straightforward example of how it's done from A to Z. I've selected a peace lily for this example since it's relatively simple to do by dividing the mother plant's sections. Let's begin!

Step 1 Check for crowns

Preferably, the mother plant should be mature enough with a healthy amount of crowns to separate. You can divide as little as three crowns for your propagation, but you could certainly try with more than that.

Step 2 Remove from pot

The next step is to take out your mother plant from its pot. Lean to one side and try to extract the plant with all its foliage together. In some cases, the plant might feel stuck, in which case the best move is to tap your pot's sides to help free it up a bit.

Step 3 Dividing

Once the plant's out of the pot, start dividing it by gently taking away a crown section from it. You can either do this by hand or carefully cut the sections off using a knife. Make sure your crown has at least two leaves with roots attached as that's necessary for successful propagation.

Step 4 Preparation

Now it's time to prepare for potting. If all goes well, you'll have to report not just the mother plant, but also the little guys you'll get through propagation!

Check the foliage and roots of them all and get rid of those brown tips on the leaves. Also, snip away any loose parts you find of the roots. With that out of the way, you're all set for potting.

Step 5 Potting

You'll need a bunch of four-inch pots depending on how many plants you're potting. Fill them with a well-draining potting mix, preferably peat-based. If it's already moist, you don't need to water it initially. But not all soil comes moistened out of the pack, so if that's the case, water it thoroughly.

Step 6 You're all done!

You're all done! All that's left to do is to arrange some aftercare for your plants. Peace lilies, in particular, thrive in bright light and a thorough watering schedule. They also need to be fed once every 35 weeks, but you won't need any additional fertilizer for at least the next couple of months or so.

Propagate Offsets & Plantlets

Hey there, plant lovers! Have you ever noticed small new plants growing from the base or sides of your mature houseplants? If so, you might have come across "plantlets" or "offsets," which are tiny new plants that have sprouted from the parent plant.

These little guys are a great way to propagate your houseplants and grow new plants for yourself or to share with friends.

Plantlets and offsets:

Plantlets and offsets are one of the easiest and most successful methods of propagating certain houseplants. They are basically small, baby plants that grow naturally from the roots or stems of the parent plant. Once they have grown a bit and developed their own root system, you can separate them from the parent plant and transplant them to create new plants.

What are plantlets and offsets?

Plantlets and offsets are essentially new plants that grow from the base or sides of a mature plant. They may look like miniature versions of the parent plant or have slightly different characteristics. Plantlets typically have their own miniature root system, while offsets may still be attached to the parent plant's root system.

Suitable Houseplants for This Method of Propagation

Plantlets and offsets are suitable for propagating certain types of plants that naturally produce new growth from the base or sides of the parent plant. These include:

- **Spider plants:** Spider plants are known for producing long, arching stems with small, baby spider plants growing from the tips. These plantlets can be propagated by simply snipping them off and planting them in a fresh potting mix.
- **Mother-in-law's tongue:** Mother-in-law's tongue or snake plants produce offsets that grow from the base of the plant. These offsets can be carefully removed and planted in their own pots.
- **African violets:** African violets produce small plantlets or "pups" that grow from the base of the leaves. These can be carefully removed and propagated into new plants.
- **Bromeliads:** Many species of bromeliads produce offsets, known as "pups," that grow from the base of the

plant. You simply need to separate these and plant them in some fresh potting mix to grow into new plants.

- **Cacti and succulents:** Some species of cacti and succulents produce offsets or small "chicks" that grow from the base of the parent plant, which makes this plant a suitable candidate for propagating via offsets. One example is the good old aloe plant!

Overall, plantlets and offsets are best for propagating plants that naturally produce new growth from the base or sides of the parent plant. This method of propagation is relatively easy and successful, making it a popular choice among houseplant enthusiasts.

Steps to propagate offsets and plantlets:

1. Identify healthy and well-established offsets or plantlets growing from the parent plant.
2. Carefully separate the plantlet or offset from the parent plant, taking care not to damage the root system. Clean off any soil or residue with clean tepid water.
3. Prepare a small pot or container with fresh, well-draining potting mix.
4. Plant the offset or plantlet into the potting mix, ensuring that the roots are covered and the plant is stable.
5. Water the newly planted offset or plantlet gently, and place it in a bright, indirect light spot.
6. Keep the soil moist but not waterlogged, and provide appropriate care for the specific houseplant species.

Tips

Before we move on, here are 5 pro tips for propagating offsets and plantlets:

1. **Be patient:** Propagating plantlets and offsets can take time, so be patient and don't rush the process. Some plantlets may take weeks or even months to develop their own root system and start growing.
2. **Use well-draining soil:** It's important to use well-draining soil when propagating plantlets and offsets. This helps prevent the roots from sitting in water and potentially rotting. Consider mixing regular potting soil with sand or perlite to improve drainage.
3. **Keep the soil moist:** While you don't want to overwater your new plantlets and offsets, it's important to keep the soil moist so that the roots can establish themselves. Water them sparingly, but regularly, and avoid letting the soil dry out completely.
4. **Provide adequate light:** Most plantlets and offsets will need bright, indirect light to grow and thrive. Avoid placing them in direct sunlight, which can scorch the leaves and damage the plant.
5. **Keep an eye out for pests:** Pests like mealybugs and spider mites can quickly take hold of new plantlets and offsets, so be sure to keep an eye out for any signs of infestation. Regularly inspect your plants and treat any pests quickly to prevent them from spreading.

Now, let's have a look at the complete process of propagating an aloe vera plant with this method from start to finish!

1. **Remove the plant from the pot:** Start by carefully removing the aloe vera plant from its pot, gently loosening the soil from around the roots. Be careful not to damage the roots or leaves during this process.

2. **Separate offsets:** Once you've removed the parent plant, look for small plantlets growing at the base of the plant. These are the offsets. Gently separate them using a clean, sharp knife or scissors. Make sure to keep some of the root system intact with the offsets, as this will help them establish themselves when planted.

3. **Remove unhealthy leaves:** Take a close look at the parent plant and remove any unhealthy or damaged leaves. You can do this by gently pulling them off the plant with your fingers or by using a clean, sharp pair of scissors. Removing unhealthy leaves will help prevent the spread of disease and encourage new growth.

4. **Remove offsets:** If there are too many offsets or you want to encourage more growth on the parent plant, you can remove some of the larger offsets. Simply twist them gently until they snap off. However, be careful not to damage the parent plant in the process.

5. **Planting:** Fill a new pot with a well-draining soil mix. Aloe vera plants do well in sandy or cactus soil, so make sure the soil is

6. porous and allows for good drainage. Make a small hole in the soil for each offset, and gently place them into the

hole. Pack the soil around the base of the offsets, making sure they are stable and not wobbling.

7. **Watering:** After planting, give the offsets a good watering. Be careful not to overwater, as aloe vera plants are susceptible to root rot. Wait until the soil is completely dry before watering again. A good rule of thumb is to water once a week during the summer months and once every two weeks in the winter.

8. **Propagating Cuttings:** In addition to offsets, aloe vera plants can also be propagated using cuttings. To do this, simply cut a healthy leaf from the parent plant and allow it to dry for a day or two. Once the cut has calloused over, plant the leaf in well-draining soil and water lightly. Within a few weeks, new roots should begin to form, and a brand new plant will start to grow!

AIR LAYERING

What is Air Layering?

Air layering is a technique used to propagate woody plants, such as trees and shrubs, by creating new roots while the plant is still attached to the parent plant. In the case of houseplants, the most suitable candidates would be large-stemmed plants that become leggy as they grow. The method involves making a small cut in the stem of the plant, wrapping it with a moist medium, and allowing new roots to grow from the wound.

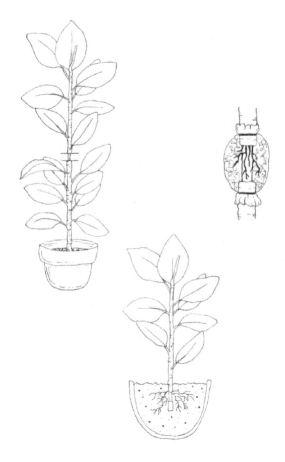

Rooting hormones

Rooting hormones are often used in air layering to stimulate the growth of new roots from the cut area of the stem. Synthetic auxins, such as IBA and NAA, are the most commonly used ones. You could determine the appropriate concentration of these hormones based on the plant species being propagated. Consult the label for expert guidance on how much of these rooting hormones to use for your particular houseplant.

Powder forms of the hormone are preferred for layering, as they're easier to apply. To use, dust the cut area of the stem with a small amount of the powder, being careful not to over-apply.

Store rooting hormones in their original containers in a cool, dark place and replace them after approximately two years as their efficacy drops over time.

What Type of Plants Is It Best For?

As a propagation technique, air layering is particularly useful for plants with a flexible stem, which allows for the creation of a wound that can be used to stimulate root growth. Also, plants that are actively growing tend to be more responsive to air layering, as they have a higher concentration of organic auxins, which are hormones that stimulate root development.

Air layering has also shown to be an effective method for propagating plants that have a low success rate with other propagation techniques, as it allows for the development of a strong root system before separating the new plant from the parent plant. Some examples of plants that are well-suited for air layering include goosefoot/syngonium, ivy, pothos, magnolia, and spider plant, as they are difficult to propagate from cuttings and have a low success rate with other propagation methods. By using air layering, you can easily boost your chances of success, hopefully resulting in healthier and more robust new plants.

Examples of Suitable Plants

Spider Plant

Spider plants are easy to propagate through offsets, but air layering can be useful for creating fuller, more mature plants. It allows for the development of multiple roots along the stem, resulting in a larger and a more established root system for the new plant. Also, spider plants have flexible stems that can be easily bent for air layering.

Goosefoot/Syngonium

Air layering is ideal for propagating goosefoot/syngonium because these plants have soft, flexible stems that are easy to manipulate to create a wound for root formation. Plus, these plants can be slow to root from stem cuttings, making air layering a more reliable, efficient, and successful method for propagating goosefoot.

Ivy

Ivy is a trailing plant that can be difficult to propagate from stem cuttings because they are slow to root and can easily rot. The air layering method has a much higher success rate for this plant as the new plant can develop a healthy root system before it gets separated from the parent Ivy.

Steps to Layering

Layering is a propagation technique that involves bending a stem to the ground or a pot, creating a wound, and allowing roots to form before cutting the stem from the parent plant. There are several different methods of layering, including simple layering, compound layering, and air layering. Here are the basic steps for each type of layering:

For Dicots

If you want to propagate your favorite dicots like the weeping fig, rubber tree, fiddle-leaf fig, or croton, then air layering might be the way to go! Here are some simple steps to follow.

First, grab a sharp knife and cut all the way around the stem you want to propagate. Remember to cut deep enough to reach the woody center of the stem.

Next, about an inch below the first cut, make another complete cut around the stem. Then, connect the two cuts with a third cut to create a ring of bark that you can remove.

After removing the ring of bark, it's time to prepare the exposed surface for rooting. Use your knife or a scraper to gently remove any soft (cambial) tissue that may still be left on the surface. This will help ensure that the air layer produces roots successfully.

That's it! You're well on your way to propagating your dicots by air layering. Just wrap the area in moist sphagnum moss and cover it with plastic wrap to create a humid environment that encourages rooting.

For Monocots

First, you'll need a sharp knife. Make an upward-slanting cut into the stem, making sure not to cut all the way through or break it off. The cut should go about one-third of the way into the stem's diameter.

Next, insert a toothpick into the cut to keep it open. Then, apply a small amount of rooting hormone to the exposed surface or push it into the cut.

Now it's time to prepare the sphagnum moss. Use about one or two handfuls of un-milled, moist sphagnum moss and wrap it around the exposed area of the stem. Make sure none of the moss is sticking out of the ends of the plastic wrap.

Wrap a piece of clear plastic around the sphagnum moss and secure it with twist ties, electrical tape, or cotton string. If you don't have clear plastic, aluminum foil or plastic wrap will work as well.

After several weeks or even months, you should see roots growing in the sphagnum moss. If the moss feels dry to the touch or gets lighter in color, add some moisture by removing the top twist-tie and pouring a little water on the moss.

Once a good root system has developed, cut off the stem just below the bottom twist tie. Then, remove the twist ties and plastic sheet and plant the rooted stem in a container using a commercial potting mix.

Make sure to keep the new plant well-watered and in bright, indirect light. Within a few weeks, the plant should be well-established and ready to be moved to its preferred location indoors.

Once the plant is established in its new container, begin regular fertilization. And that's it - you've successfully propagated a new monocot plant by air layering!

Simple Layering

First, take a stem or branch and bend or stretch it down to the soil or over to an adjacent container with potting soil or rooting media like perlite or sphagnum moss.

Next, bury the stem 24 inches deep, making sure that at least one (if not more) node is buried. Be sure not to bury any leaves, and remove any leaves that would be buried in the rooting media.

To help hold the stem in place, you can pin it down with floral pins, hairpins, or a bent paper clip. If you want faster root development, you can try wounding the branch and dusting it with rooting hormone powder before burying it.

Now, be patient and wait for 6 to 12 weeks (or maybe longer, depending on the species) for new roots to form. Once the stem is firmly rooted into the soil, you can cut or separate it from the parent plant.

If you used rooting media like perlite, be sure to pot the new plant in regular potting soil. Once potted, keep it well-watered and in bright, indirect light. Within a few weeks, the plant should be well established and can be moved to its preferred location indoors.

Don't forget to begin regular fertilization once the plant is established! And if you're propagating from a parent plant, it can be allowed to grow once the propagule is removed. Most plants will break buds just below the cut and create several new branches. If it's no longer desired, the parent plant can be discarded.

Seed Sowing

Seed sowing, the last propagation method covered in this chapter, is comparatively more complex. As the name suggests, it involves directly growing plants from the seeds.

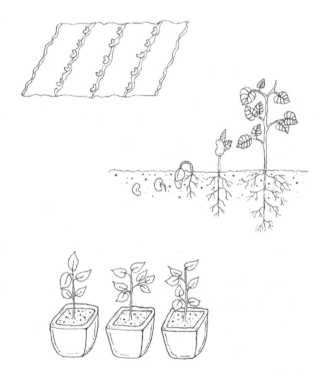

It takes more time and also needs a particular set of environmental conditions to work well, which are prerequisites that aren't easily manageable for the average houseplant parent. That's why usually only professional growers and nurseries use it. But, that doesn't mean you can't give it a shot!

Steps to Growing From Seeds

You can easily find and order seeds for your desired plants online. The strelitzia reginae or solanum capsicastrum, for instance, would be some good seeds to get your hands on to try it out.

Once you've got your seeds, place them on top of the soil with some space between each one. Do this in a tray or a pot with a plastic covering on it. Water it thoroughly and put a compost layer on seeds that are somewhat larger. This tray or container ideally needs a warm environment of about 70 degrees Fahrenheit and very little light. A spacious cupboard, for instance, wouldn't be a bad spot as long as it's warm enough.

Wait for the seeds to germinate and once you see some signs of growth breaking out from the top layer of your soil, then it's time to remove the cover and bring the container out into a brighter location without any direct sunlight.

Even though the process is a bit trickier, it can still be a fun and educational way to experiment for you and your kids. Who knows, you might even ace it on your first try!

Tips

Here are some tips for you to increase your success rate when propagating plants by sowing seeds:

- **Choose the right type of compost:** It's important to use a good quality compost that is suitable for seed sowing. Look for one that's specifically labeled as seed compost or fine seed compost, as these have the right texture and nutrients for seedlings. Avoid using heavy or nutrient-rich compost, as this can be too strong for young plants.

- **Build in drainage:** Proper drainage is crucial for seed sowing success. Make sure the container you use has drainage holes to prevent waterlogging. You can also add a layer of gravel or perlite at the bottom of the container to improve drainage.

- **Consider using pelleted seeds:** Pelleted seeds are coated in a layer of clay, which makes them easier to handle and sow. This can be a particularly helpful life hack if you're new to seed sowing or have difficulty with fine seeds.

- **Use a windowsill for propagation:** A sunny windowsill can provide the perfect conditions for seedlings to thrive. Make sure the windowsill is warm and receives plenty of natural light, and protect your seedlings from cold drafts.

- **Space out your seeds:** It's important to give your seeds enough space to grow into healthy plants. Follow the recommended spacing guidelines for the specific plant you're sowing, and avoid overcrowding your container. Thin out any seedlings that are too close together to prevent competition for nutrients.

By following these tips, you can improve your chances of success when propagating plants by sowing seeds.

Propagating Tips and Tricks

Having covered some of the most popular ways of propagating houseplants, let's look at some individual propagation tips and tricks that you can use to boost your chances of success!

Getting a cutting in the mail

Don't be afraid to order cuttings online. Getting a cutting in the mail can be a great way to expand your plant collection, but it can also be intimidating. Don't worry - as long as you handle the cutting with care, it should be just fine. When you receive the cutting, unwrap it gently and inspect it for any signs of damage. If it looks healthy, you can move on to rooting it.

Rooted vs unrooted

Rooted cuttings have already developed roots and are ready to be planted, while unrooted cuttings need to be rooted first. Rooted cuttings are often more expensive than unrooted ones, but they're also less risky since they're more likely to survive.

If you've been struggling to get your cuttings to root, try using rooting hormone. This product contains hormones that encourage root growth, making it easier for your cuttings to take hold. Simply dip the cut end of your cutting in the hormone and plant it as usual.

How to root a cutting

When you're rooting a cutting, it's important to keep the soil moist so that the roots can develop. But with that said, you definitely don't want to overwater your cutting, as this can lead to root rot. Try misting the cutting with a spray bottle, or placing it in a clear plastic bag to increase humidity.

Rooting hormone can also be a game-changer. If you're struggling to get your cuttings to root, try using rooting hormone. This product contains hormones that encourage root growth, making it easier for your cuttings to take hold. Simply dip the cut end of your cutting in the hormone and plant it as usual.

Recreate the environment (heat mats work wonders!)

Cuttings need the right environment to root and grow into strong plantlets. Use a heat mat to speed up the rooting process. Most plants need warm temperatures to root successfully, and a heat mat can help provide just the right conditions.

Simply place your cutting on the heat mat and adjust the temperature as needed. Make sure to keep an eye on the soil moisture, as heat can cause the soil to dry out more quickly.

Care after rooting

After your cutting has rooted, it's important to continue caring for it properly to ensure it thrives. Monitor the soil moisture and adjust watering as needed, and fertilize the plant with a balanced fertilizer every few weeks. Keep an eye out for any signs of disease or pest infestations, and address them promptly if they occur.

Choose the right potting mix for your plant. Different plants have different soil requirements, so you have to choose a mix that's just right for the type of cutting you're working with. Some plants prefer well-draining soil, while others need a more moisture-retentive mix. Do your research and choose a potting mix that'll give your cutting the best chance of success.

Getting your cutting to callous

This might sound like a strange step, but it's actually really important! When you take a cutting from a plant, the end of the stem is exposed and vulnerable to disease and rot. To prevent this from happening, you'll want to let the cut end dry out and form a callous before you try to root it. This can take anywhere from a few hours to a few days, depending on the plant and the conditions.

Once the cut end is dry and calloused, you can proceed with rooting the cutting.

Warmer temperature over more light

When it comes to rooting cuttings, warmth is more important than light. While some light is necessary for the process, what your cuttings really need is warmth and humidity. You can create a mini-greenhouse for your cuttings by placing them in a clear plastic bag or container with some moist soil or rooting hormone. Then, find a warm spot for them to sit, like on top of the fridge or near a heat vent. They'll love the cozy environment, and you'll love how quickly they start to root!

Using root and grow solution

If you're really serious about propagating plants, you might want to invest in a root and grow solution. These products contain hormones and nutrients that can help your cuttings develop strong roots and establish themselves more quickly. Simply dip the cut end of your cutting in the solution before planting it in soil or another rooting medium. Follow the instructions on the package, and you'll be amazed at how quickly your cuttings start to grow!

Using filtered water

Finally, if you're having trouble getting your cuttings to root, it might be time to look at the water you're using. Tap water can contain chlorine and other chemicals that can be harmful to plants. Instead, try using filtered water. This can be water that you've run through a filter pitcher, a reverse osmosis system, or even just water that you've let sit out for a day or two to let the chlorine dissipate. Your cuttings will thank you for the extra care!

Keep your tools clean

When you're taking cuttings from a plant, it's important to keep your tools clean and sterile. This can help prevent the spread of disease

and make it easier for the cuttings to root. Use a clean, sharp pair of scissors or pruning shears to take your cuttings, and disinfect them between each cutting. You can use rubbing alcohol or a diluted bleach solution to clean your tools.

Don't give up too soon

Finally, it's important to be patient when you're propagating plants. It can take several weeks or even months for cuttings to start growing roots and developing into new plants. Don't give up if you don't see immediate results - keep providing your cuttings with the right conditions and care, and they'll eventually start to grow. And remember, even if some of your cuttings don't make it, you can always learn from your mistakes and try again - that's the beauty of gardening!

And speaking of mistakes, Let's round this chapter up with a few propagation blunders to avoid...

Propagation Mistakes to Avoid

Using the wrong compost

Using the right compost is essential for successful plant propagation. If you use the wrong type of compost, your cuttings might not root properly and potentially even fail to survive. When you're propagating plants, you can barely go wrong with using a light, sterile compost that drains well.

Avoid using heavy or compacted soils, as they can retain too much water and cause your cuttings to root. It's also a good idea to use a compost that has a low nutrient content since too many nutrients can actually harm your cuttings. You can either make your own compost or buy a commercially available seed or cutting compost. Whatever you choose, make sure it's appropriate for the type of plant you're propagating.

Allowing plants to dehydrate

When you take a cutting from a plant, you've got to keep it moist until it starts to root. I've reiterated this quite a few times throughout this chapter, but it's simply that important.

If the cutting dries out, it won't be able to develop roots and will likely die. To prevent this from happening, you should keep your cuttings in a humid environment, such as under a clear plastic bag or in a propagator. Make sure the compost stays moist but not waterlogged, and mist the cuttings regularly to keep them hydrated.

Dividing overly small root balls

When you're dividing plants, you must make sure each division has a sufficient root ball. If you divide a plant that has an overly small root ball, the roots might not be able to support the plant properly leading to a failed propagation attempt. To avoid this, make sure each division has a good amount of roots attached. If you're not sure, you can gently tug on the plant to see if it's firmly rooted in the soil.

Using the wrong propagation methods

There are many different ways to propagate plants, but not all methods work for every type of plant. For example, some plants might do better with stem cuttings, while others might prefer leaf cuttings or division. Before you start propagating a plant, do some research to find out what method works best for that particular type of plant. Using the wrong method could result in failure or even unnecessary harm to the plant.

Planting out too soon

When your cuttings or seedlings start to develop roots or new growth, it can be tempting to plant them out in the garden right away. However, it's important to wait until they're strong enough to survive in their new environment. If you plant them out too soon, they might not be able to handle the shock of the new conditions and could die. Make sure your plants are well established and have developed a strong root system before planting them out.

Not providing your plants with enough light

Like heat and humidity, light is also essential for plant growth. If your cuttings or seedlings don't get enough light, they'll struggle to grow and may not make it. To give them enough light to thrive, you can place them near a sunny window, use grow lights, or even take them outside on sunny days (only recommended for species that are safe to be exposed to direct sunlight).

If your plants start to look pale or leggy, they might not be getting enough light and you'll need to adjust their environment.

FINAL TAKEAWAY

So there we have it. We've gone over everything you need to know to start your journey as a propagation champ. This chapter — being by far the longest one in this book — has covered the methods, tips, and the complete ins and outs of propagation. It's a phenomenal concept of creating new plant life and once you master it, you'll unlock the ability to expand your collection without spending a single penny or leaving the house.

But, now that you know how to propagate, the next question is — **what to propagate?** That's exactly what's waiting for you in the next chapter. I've divided my picks into categories of easy, hard, and rare to make sure there's an exciting propagation project in store for you regardless of your skill level!

5

PLANTS TO PROPAGATE: EASY, HARD, & RARE

As we've already learned in the previous chapters, there are several methods for propagating plants and expanding your collection. Some are easier than others with a higher success rate, while others require conditions that aren't easily achievable. Similarly, the plants you choose to propagate will also play a role in how easy the process is going to be as well as your chances of getting it right.

As a beginner with no prior experience in propagation, picking the easiest propagation method and plant makes the most sense, right? As you grow your skill and gain more confidence, you can move on to plants that are relatively harder to propagate. Once you've got a few of those down and still want to keep exploring, I'd then suggest trying to propagate some rarer plants to diversify the look of your houseplant collection.

If that's the type of model you're looking to follow, this chapter will certainly help you plan out the roadmap of your propagation adventures. I've categorized plants that are easy, hard, and rare when it comes to propagation.

Rarer ones, of course, cost more to propagate (or even attempt to do so) since the cuttings don't come cheap. You certainly don't want to use them as your "experiment batch." Once you completely understand the basics and have some practical experience under your belt, feel free to venture onto exotic plants. Having a healthy mix of normal and rare plants creates a colorful contrast that accentuates the aesthetics of your house-plant display.

Your choice of rare plants is also a great opportunity to add a distinctive touch to your collection. That's because every houseplant parent is likely to have their hands on some aloe, pothos, or spider plants, but if you've got something like a white princess or a variegated syngonium in the mix, that'll set the look apart.

So without further ado, let's have a look at these plants, how to propagate them, and tips for success with each one.

EASY PLANTS TO PROPAGATE

Let's start with the easiest of the lot. These are the ideal plant species to propagate if you don't have much experience and want to have some room for error in the process. Not only are these plants easy to propagate, but also cheap to find cuttings or seeds for, making them the ideal candidates for your first few digs at this practice.

1. Rosemary

Rosemary Salvia rosmarinus) is a woody, perennial herb that is commonly used in cooking and aromatherapy. If you want to propagate rosemary, one of the easiest ways to do it is through stem cuttings. Start by selecting a healthy, non-flowering stem from your rosemary plant. Make a clean cut at a 45-degree angle with a sharp pair of pruning shears, just below a leaf node.

Next, remove the lower leaves from the stem, leaving only a few leaves at the top. Dip the cut end of the stem into rooting hormone powder to promote root growth. Then, plant the stem in a container filled with well-draining potting soil. Keep the soil moist, but not overly wet, and place the container in a warm and bright location, but not in direct sunlight.

Within a few weeks, the cutting should start to develop roots and new growth. Once the roots have grown long enough, you can transplant your new rosemary plant into a larger container or into your garden. With proper care, your new rosemary plant will flourish and provide you with fresh, aromatic leaves for all your culinary needs.

2. Tradescantia

Tradescantia is a beautiful plant that is also known as the Wandering Jew or Spiderwort. If you have a Tradescantia plant and you want to propagate it, there are a few different methods you can try. One of the easiest ways is by taking stem cuttings.

To get started, choose a healthy stem from your plant and use a pair of sharp scissors to make a clean cut just below a node. Nodes are the points on the stem where leaves emerge. Once you have your cutting, remove any leaves from the bottom half of the stem.

Next, dip the cut end of the stem into some rooting hormone powder. This will help stimulate root growth. Then, plant the stem in a container filled with moist potting soil. Make sure to water the soil regularly, so it stays moist but not waterlogged.

In a few weeks, you should start to see new growth on your cutting, which means that roots have formed. Once the roots are well-established, you can transplant your new Tradescantia plant into a larger pot or your garden. They'll be sure to add a pop of color wherever you decide to put them!

3. Prayer Plant

The Prayer Plant Maranta leuconeura) is a beautiful and popular houseplant that gets its name from the way its leaves fold up at night like hands in prayer. If you want to propagate your Prayer Plant, there are a few different methods you can try. One of the easiest and most reliable ways is through division.

To propagate your Prayer Plant through division, start by gently removing the plant from its pot and carefully separating the root ball into smaller sections. Each section should have a healthy amount of roots and a few stems with leaves. If you have any dead or damaged roots or leaves, make sure to remove them before dividing the plant.

Once you've divided your Prayer Plant, plant each section into its own pot with fresh, well-draining soil. Make sure to water the soil thoroughly after planting, and then keep the soil moist but not soggy. Prayer Plants prefer bright, indirect light, so find a spot in your home where they can get enough light without being exposed to direct sunlight.

4. Umbrella Plant

The Umbrella Plant (Schefflera arboricola) is a tropical houseplant that is easy to care for and can be propagated through stem cuttings. If you have an Umbrella Plant that you want to propagate, here's what you need to do:

Start by selecting a healthy stem from your plant. Make sure it's at least 46 inches long and has a few leaves on it. Using a sharp pair of scissors or pruning shears, make a clean cut at a 45-degree angle just below a node. Nodes are the points on the stem where leaves emerge.

Next, remove the lower leaves from the stem, leaving only a few at the top. This will help reduce the amount of moisture lost through the leaves, and allow the plant to focus on developing roots. Dip the cut end of the stem into rooting hormone powder, which will help stimulate root growth.

Now, plant the stem in a pot filled with moist, well-draining soil. You can use a small pot or container, as the Umbrella Plant doesn't require a lot of space when it's young. Make sure to water the soil thoroughly, and then keep it moist but not water-logged. Cover the pot with a plastic bag or wrap to help retain moisture and create a humid environment.

New growth should start popping up in a few weeks. Once the roots seem strong enough, feel free to move the cutting into a large pot of its own!

5. Pothos

Pothos plants are some of the hardiest ones out there, giving you all the cushion you need as a beginner caregiver. Not only are they easy to maintain, but also to propagate! They root well under water so the best way to multiply your collection is to put some cuttings in water.

To do that, spot a new leaf sprouting out and cut the vine just underneath that point. Then, grab a pair of clean, sharp scissors and inflict a cut on either of the node's sides. Space the cut about half an inch away from the node. Once you've made clean cuts on the left and right of every node, you should be left with a total of five or six cuttings to work with.

Simply put all of these in a jar of water and wait. In a couple of weeks, new roots should start to develop. Once they're about an inch long, it's time to move them into fresh soil in a new pot!

6. Sansevieria

Sansevieria, also known as Snake Plant, is a popular houseplant that is loved for its hardiness and unique appearance. If you have a Sansevieria plant and want to propagate it, there are a few different methods you can try. One of the easiest and fastest ways is through division.

To propagate your Sansevieria through division, start by removing the plant from its pot and gently separating the root ball into smaller sections. Remember to get rid of any dead or damaged roots or leaves before dividing the plant. Once you've divided your Sansevieria, plant each section into its own pot with fresh, well-draining soil. Make sure to water the soil thoroughly after planting, and then keep the soil slightly moist.

Another way to propagate Sansevieria is through leaf cuttings. To do this, simply take a healthy leaf from your Sansevieria plant and put it in a glass of water. Make sure the leaf is partially submerged in the water and that the container is in a warm area with indirect light. Change the water every few days, and wait for roots to develop. Once the leaf has developed roots, you can transfer it to a pot with well-draining soil. With a little patience and care, you should have a new Sansevieria plant in no time.

7. Spider plant

Spider plants (Chlorophytum comosum) are known for their long, thin leaves that grow from a central rosette and produce plantlets or "spiderettes" at the end of long, wiry stems. If you want to propagate your spider plant, there are a few different methods you can try.

One of the easiest ways to propagate your spider plant is through the plantlets that grow from the mother plant. These plantlets can be left on the mother plant until they start to develop roots or can be carefully removed and planted in their own pots. Once the plantlets have developed roots, they can be transplanted into their own pots with fresh potting soil.

Another way to propagate spider plants is through stem cuttings. To do this, select a healthy stem and make a clean cut just below a node using a sharp pair of scissors or pruning shears. Remove any leaves from the lower part of the stem, leaving a few at the top. Dip the cut end of the stem into rooting hormone powder and plant the stem in a pot with moist potting soil. Keep the soil moist and in a bright, indirect light location until the stem has developed roots and new growth appears.

8. ZZ Plant

Zamioculcas zamiifolia, or ZZ plant for short, is another popular houseplant having shiny, dark green leaves and super easy care requirements. If you've got one already and want to propagate it, you can do so by division or through stem cuttings.

For **division**, gently remove the plant from its pot and carefully separate the root ball into smaller sections — each having a few leaves and a healthy amount of roots. Use a clean and sharp tool to avoid damaging the roots. Once you've divided your ZZ plant, plant each section into its own pot with fresh potting soil. Water the soil thoroughly after planting, and then keep the soil slightly moist.

Another way to propagate ZZ plants is through **leaf cuttings**. To do this, select a healthy leaf from your ZZ plant and make a clean cut at the base of the leaf using a sharp pair of scissors or pruning shears. Place the leaf in a glass of water or directly into moist potting soil. Make sure the container is in a warm, bright area but not in direct sunlight. Wait for the roots to develop, and once they have, you can transfer the new plant into a pot with fresh potting soil.

9. Chinese Money Plant

Interestingly enough, the Chinese Money Plant is one of the easiest to propagate out of all other plant species. That's because it naturally does it for you! If you've recently bought this plant or simply have one growing in your garden, just wait for it to pop up some babies by itself. Let them grow to a height of about 2 or 3 inches and then remove and repot them in fresh soil. As long as the babies have enough root systems to support them, you don't need to do anything else.

10. String of Pearls

Here we have another plant that "self-propagates" in a way. Although the process isn't the same as the Chinese money plant above, it's arguably more miraculous.

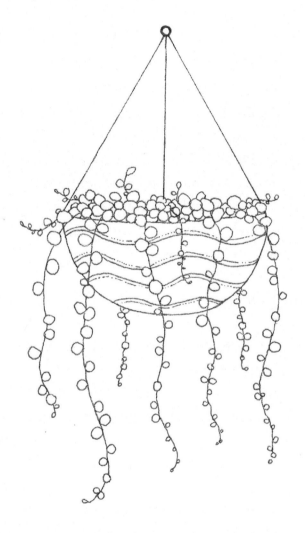

Suppose you have a String of Pearls plant in a hanging basket. To propagate the plant, take a new pot and fill it with your preferred potting soil. Then, place the potting soil beneath your String of Pearls and cover it with a layer of soil. By placing the hanging parts of the plant onto the soil bed, new roots will eventually sprout. In the meantime, make sure to water the compost as you would for other propagation methods. After roughly four weeks, new roots should have developed, and you can then detach (cut) the mother plant from the new plant and repot it. Cool, right?

11. String of Bananas

The String of Bananas, a vine plant similar to the String of Pearls, can also be propagated using the method described above. To propagate your String of Bananas, layer the plant's end on a fresh pot with potting soil and wait for the roots to form. The process should take about four weeks.

If all this seems "too easy" to believe, don't worry, that's how this list is supposed to be. Harder ones are waiting for you later on in the chapter!

12. String of Hearts

String of Hearts — also known as Chain of Hearts — is another trailing plant that's native to Africa. It has some succulent-like properties that make it super resilient and easy to care for. To multiply it, you could either propagate it directly in soil or in the water. Both have a pretty high success rate but I personally find the water route slightly simpler overall.

Here are the steps to water-propagate your String of Hearts:

1. Select a healthy string of hearts planted with long vines and cut a few strands near the leaf nodes using a clean and sharp pair of scissors or pruning shears. Make sure each cutting is at least two to three inches long and has a few leaves.

2. Fill a clean jar or vase with distilled or filtered water. You can also use tap water, but let it sit for 24 hours to allow any chlorine to dissipate.

3. Place the cuttings into the jar or vase of water, making sure the bottom of each cutting is submerged in the water.

4. Place the jar or vase in a bright location, but out of direct sunlight. String of Hearts prefers bright but indirect light.

5. Change the water every week or when it appears dirty or cloudy. Make sure to rinse the cuttings under running water before putting them back in the jar.

6. In about 4-6 weeks, you should notice roots developing from the bottom of each cutting. When the roots are at least one inch long, you can transplant the cuttings into a pot with well-draining soil.

7. Once the new plant has established itself in the soil, you can begin to care for it as you would with any other String of Hearts plant.

13. Moses in the Cradle

Just like the ZZ plant, Moses in the Cradle — or Tradescantia Spathacea — can also be propagated easily through two methods: stem cuttings or division. The process is very similar for these two plants and they're equally simple to care for as well.

Simply remove some offshoots that pop up around mature plants and pot them individually. Just make sure that the roots are attached when you pot these plantlets.

14. Arrowhead Plant

Here's another easy-to-propagate houseplant that can really fill up the look of your houseplant display. With its large and wide leaves, the arrowhead plant can really add a touch of character in any indoor space.

It naturally roots well in water, so the simplest way to multiply your collection would be to take some healthy stem cuttings and place them in water. You don't even need to use any rooting hormone on these as the plant has a high tendency to produce roots by itself.

15. Strawberry Begonia (Saxifraga stolonifera)

Strawberry Begonia (Saxifraga stolonifera) is a charming trailing plant that gets its name from the small, strawberry-like plantlets that grow along its thin stems. If you have a Strawberry Begonia and would like to propagate it, there are a few different methods you can try.

One of the easiest ways to propagate a Strawberry Begonia is through the plantlets that grow on its stems. Simply wait for the plantlets to form roots and then gently separate them from the parent plant using a clean pair of scissors or pruning shears. Plant the new plantlet in a small pot with fresh, well-draining soil and keep the soil slightly moist but not too wet. Place the pot in a bright, indirect light location and wait for new growth to appear.

16. Peperomia Hope

Peperomia hope (Peperomia rotundifolia) is a delightful, beginner-friendly houseplant. Every part of this plant can multiply your collection through propagation. We're talking stems, leaves, or even just a part of a leaf. Just stick your cuttings or stems into water or slightly moist potting soil and wait. Roots should start to form in a couple of weeks — simple as that!

17. Polka Dot Begonia (Begonia maculata)

Want to add a statement piece to your houseplant collection? Why not expand your family of the Polka Dot Begonia plant? The white dots on its leaves, as well as the fully red underside, can give you all the pop you need for your aesthetic display.

Despite looking like a rare plant, the polka dot begonia is super easy to propagate. Just snip a piece off with the leaf and node attached, and put the cutting into a jar of water. Roots should start to form after two or three weeks, allowing you to transfer the rooted cutting into a mix of loamy soil and sandy clay.

18. Hardy Elephant Ear (Alocasia wentii)

The Hardy Elephant Ear, like most other Alocasia plants, is super easy to propagate as it virtually does it on its own. The plant grows tubers underground, from which new plants naturally pop up.

You've simply got to remove the mother plant from the pot and dig out the soil where you see pups emerging. These will be attached to the rhizome and will probably already be rooting, so all that's left to do is remove a section with leaves and pot it separately with some soil — and you're done!

HARD TO PROPAGATE HOUSEPLANTS

Now that we've gone over quite a few plants that are super easy to propagate, let's now look at plants that pose a little bit of a challenge when you want to multiply them. If you've already tried and found success with your propagation attempts with the above plants, you're hopefully ready to take on plants like the Venus flytrap, gardenia, and the moth orchid. They're a bit tricky, but follow the steps and tips shared in this section and you should be good to go.

1. Moth Orchid

Moth orchids, unlike simpler plants like the ZZ or pothos, will require a fair amount of patience on your part. That's because upon blooming, this plant will take some time to regenerate before it's ready for the next round. It drops its previous flowers to focus all the energy on producing new ones. With appropriate care, conditions, and enough patience, you can hopefully expect it to bloom twice or thrice a year. This is why, despite being relatively trickier to care for and propagate, the moth orchid is still a worthwhile plant to have in your home.

Keep in mind that the orchids might not look the healthiest at the beginning of the regeneration period. Before attempting to propagate it, make sure there aren't any signs of dehydration like shriveling. If everything looks good, you can propagate the plant by division. To do so, get the orchid out from its pot and carefully pull apart the sections with each one having roots, leaves, and at least one stem attached. Plant the sections in their own individual pots with, well-draining orchid soil and water thoroughly. New plants should start to pop up in a few weeks!

2. Croton

Want some multi-colored leaves to boost the vibrancy in your houseplant display? Crotons might be exactly what you're looking for. Bear in mind though, these tropical charmers aren't the most easy-going when it comes to plant care and propagation. They don't adapt well to change and demand regular watering to thrive in an indoor environment.

When it comes to propagation, your best bet would be doing it through stem cuttings. Take one that's about three or four inches in length, ideally with three to five leaves attached to it. Grab some general rooting hormone and dip the cut end in before planting it in a smaller individual pot. Be careful not to overwater the soil but always keep it moist. Maintain the temperature at around 70 to 80 degrees Fahrenheit and if all goes well, your cuttings should root in under a month!

3. Fiddle-leaf Fig Tree

If you're a plant parent with some experience under your belt, you can't go wrong with a fiddle-leaf fig tree. This large ficus has unique paddle-shaped leaves that are large enough to fill up a corner. They are, however, sensitive to overwatering so keep your waterings light and limit them to once a week. They also need high humidity levels too, which also makes their propagation slightly tricky in indoor conditions.

To multiply your collection, I find propagating this plant through stem cuttings the easiest. Snip a stem with two or three leaves attached, cutting about three inches below the first leaf. Dip it in some off-the-shelf rooting powder and immediately submerge in some chlorine-free water. Place the container in a bright spot without any direct sunlight and wait. In three weeks, you should be able to spot some roots forming. Let them grow for another week and once they look healthy enough, replant them into a new pot with some fresh, well-draining potting mix.

4. Bird's Nest Fern

The bird's nest fern is a distinct-looking plant thanks to its unique, curly texture and bright green color. It does require frequent watering, though, so if you tend to often forget doing that as a plant parent, this one might be a pass. If you're confident enough in your punctuality, however, the gorgeous aesthetics of this plant surely make it worth the effort.

If you're ready to expand your collection by propagating it, the best way is to do it through spores. Start by finding mature fronds with small, round spores on the undersides of the leaves. You can cut these fronds off and collect the spores in a paper bag. Sprinkle the spores on top of moist, well-draining soil in a pot, and cover the pot with a plastic bag to create a humid environment. Find a bright spot for your new fern babies and keep the soil consistently moist. It might take a while for the spores to germinate, but once they do, you'll see tiny ferns start to grow. It's amazing to watch them develop into beautiful, full-grown ferns that you can enjoy in your home or give to friends as a gift.

5. Boston Fern

The Boston Fern, sharing a lot of the looks and properties with the bird's nest fern discussed above, is a fairly inexpensive plant that's a promising investment from a value-for-money stand-point. As long as you maintain a healthy and consistent level of moisture and humidity, they should do just fine.

The best propagation method to multiply these, however, would be division. Similarly to the steps for division we've gone over for other plants, simply remove a large plant from its pot and prise apart the root ball gently using forks. You can also slice through it with a bread knife. Once new growth pops up with a healthy root system, pot the plants individually and water well!

6. Zebra Plant

The Zebra Plant, or the Aphelandra Squarrosa, is a tropical shrub that has a strong presence in any indoor setting. The bright white patterns on its large leaves are hard to miss, making it a fancy attention-grabber.

To propagate this plant, you should start by taking a herbaceous cutting of the mother plant. Pick a healthy stem and snip off a three to five-inch long piece with several leaves. Position your cut just below the node and get rid of any leaves at the stem's lower part, leaving a couple up top. Then, dip the cut end into some rooting hormone and pot it in some moist soil with a plastic covering on top to maintain sufficiently humid conditions. Place it in a bright spot with indirect lighting and wait for your fresh new zebra plant to grow!

7. Gardenia

If you're a fan of flowering houseplants, gardenia is a must-have. It enriches your home's ambiance with bright and fragrant white flowers in bloom season, and the beauty far outweighs its mild high-maintenance woes.

If you'd ask me, you can never have enough gardenia! Thankfully, the plant isn't too difficult to propagate if you time it right. In midsummer, the plant gives vigorous new shoots that root very easily. Snip a 5-inch section from a healthy branch tip. Trim off all the flowers and leaves from the bottom and put some rooting hormone on the cut end. Push the cutting into a peat moss and sand mixture and cover it with plastic for added humidity. Maintain a consistent level of moisture in the soil and the plant should root in no time. After about a month or so, your cutting should be ready to be moved into a larger pot of its own.

8. Cheese Plant (Monstera)

The Cheese Plant, better known as Monstera, is another promising plant to add to your collection thanks to the unique appearance of its split leaves. Thanks to its all-green aesthetic, the plant never looks tacky in any type of indoor space. But at the same time, the unique and distinctive leaves keep it far from boring as well — which is a win-win for houseplant enthusiasts.

You can propagate your monster plant using stem cuttings as well through a process that's highly similar to the one shared for the two plants above. If you choose to root the stem cutting in water, though, it'll be essential to keep changing the water every few days to keep it fresh and avoid any bacterial buildup.

9. African Mask

The African Mask, commonly known as the Kris plant, is an Alocasia type that's native to the South Pacific tropics. The foliage uniquely resembles ceremonial African masks with carved patterns, hence the curious name. You can't miss how exotic this plant looks, and it'll certainly be a conversation-starter with guests!

You can propagate the plant through division. To have the best possible shot at success, attempt it in the summer or spring season. Gently get the plant out of its pot and tease its roots apart. You can also make use of a sterile, sharp knife to get the rhizomes separated. Plant these divisions in some well-draining potting soil at the same depth and water it regularly. In the right conditions, that's all you have to do for these divisions to start growing into new, independent African Mask plants!

10. Goldfish Plant

Goldfish plant (Nematanthus) is a tropical houseplant known for its unique and colorful flowers that resemble little goldfish.

It's a relatively easy plant to care for and propagate, making it a great choice for plant enthusiasts of all levels.

You can propagate your goldfish plant through stem cuttings. Choose your best-looking stem, and cut it right at the point where the leaf meets the stem under a node. Get rid of leaves on the lower section (if any) and dip the cut end in rooting powder for faster rooting. Submerge the cutting in a jar of water and wait for the roots to grow over an inch in length. Then, plant it in some fresh potting mix and enjoy growing a brand new goldfish plant!

11. Venus Flytrap

Last on our list of houseplants that are hard to propagate, we have the Venus flytrap. It's the first and only carnivorous plant included in this book, which also makes it one of the most unique houseplants you can have in your collection. If you've already got your hands on one of these, it totally makes sense to try and multiply it!

The simplest way to propagate a Venus flytrap is through division. When you notice that your Venus flytrap has outgrown its pot, carefully remove it from the soil and gently separate the plant into two or three smaller clumps. Each clump should have a few healthy leaves and a small section of root attached.

Plant each new clump in its own pot filled with a mixture of peat moss and sand, and keep the soil moist (but not too damp). Place the new pots in a bright location with plenty of indirect sunlight. In a few months, you should start to see new growth appearing from each clump. With a little patience and care, your Venus flytrap will thrive and multiply!

RARE PLANTS TO PROPAGATE

Once you enter the world of propagation, it makes sense to start with easy plants and then multiply harder ones. Having propagated a few plants from each of the two lists above, you're now equipped with enough knowledge and experience to take a decent jab at propagating any plant you want.

If you've reached that stage, this next list is where it gets interesting. I've gathered a bunch of rare plants to propagate that'll look super impressive and exotic inside your home or office, so feel free to grab and multiply any one that catches your eye.

1. Variegated Monsteras

We've already covered one basic type of monster (the cheese plant) in the list above, but that's not the only one. Here are a few rarer ones that you can propagate!

i) Monstera deliciosa albo variegata

The deliciosa albo variegata is a variegated variant of the monstera deliciosa, and that's where the "rare" look mostly comes from. Every leaf has a unique pattern and you'll only know what it looks like once it opens up. Generally through, they consist of jade-green leaves with bright white patterns on top. Some can even be almost fully white while others have blocks, patterns, or splotches. The plant is a very slow grower which is partly why they're low in number.

They're still high in demand though, and that explains why it's so expensive!

Full plants can set you back by over $500 to even a couple thousand dollars in some parts of the world. Since that's unaffordable for many plant enthusiasts, propagating might be the only practical option to get your hands on this one or expand your collection. Just make sure to purchase a good cutting and don't get scammed! If you're ordering online, make sure to locate at least one node on the cutting. Also, the stems on genuine deliciosa albo monsteras are supposed to be variegated as well, so if you see solid green color — something's not right.

When it comes to the propagation process itself, you have some options but I'd try rooting it in water. Use chlorine-free, filtered water, and a high-quality rooting hormone to support quicker development. Keep it in a bright and warm spot with indirect lighting! Wait for root systems to branch out into smaller roots of two or more inches in length before trying to move it into its own pot. The stronger the roots, the better shot your albo will have at surviving and thriving upon transplantation.

ii) Monstera aurea variegata

The Monstera aurea variegata is very similar to the classic deliciosa above, but it's just smaller with a few distinct characteristics. As up-and-comers, they're even rarer than the classic variegated monster versions but that trend seems to be changing as their availability seems to be improving online.

Depending on maturity and size, a single one of these plants can cost you between $250 to $3,000 — which is more than many people can spare for a hobby. That's why your best bet is to find a decent cutting and propagate it in water, soil, or through air layering.

Soil would be my recommendation for this one since making the move from water to potting mix later on can be a bit of a dicey shock for this one. But with that said, many people propagate the Monstera aurea variegata in water with a high success rate so if that's the method you're most experienced in, by all means go for it.

To root the cutting in soil, however, you've simply got to stick it in a potting mix container and water it thoroughly. Feel free to use some magic powder (i.e. propagation-promoting rooting hormone) to discourage infection and boost the rooting process. You should start seeing visible root growth within a few months, allowing you to transplant it to a pot of its own! And just like that, the value of your humble little houseplant display just skyrocketed.

iii) Monstera sport

Monstera sport is a term used to describe a naturally occurring genetic mutation that results in a unique and attractive variegation pattern on the leaves of Monstera plants. This variegation can come in the form of white or yellow patches, stripes, or even polka dots, and can add a striking visual interest to your Monstera plant collection.

Propagating Monstera sports can be done through stem cuttings, just like propagating a regular Monstera plant. Look for a stem that has a variegated leaf or two on it, and cut the stem just below a node or leaf. Dip the cut end of the stem into rooting hormone powder and then plant it into a pot filled with moist soil.

Place the pot in a warm and bright location, but out of direct sunlight. Make sure to keep the soil moist but not too wet, as too much water can cause the stem to rot. After a few weeks, you should start to see new growth appearing from the cuttings. Once the cuttings have established roots and are growing well, you can transplant them into their own individual pots. With a little patience and care, you'll have a collection of unique and beautiful Monstera sports in no time!

iv) Monstera Thai Constellation

Like all the other variegated monster variants we've covered above, the Thai constellation is also hard to come by since it can't be grown from seeds. It's a newer plant and people want to get their hands on it which of course drives prices up. But thankfully, you can use the propagation skills you've garnered to save up hundreds of dollars by rooting a cutting and growing your plant from scratch.

During the growing season find a healthy-looking Thai Constellation stem cutting having at least one leaf and a node. Be careful, a cutting without a node **will not root** no matter how pretty it looks in the photos or IRL. Now, the plant is naturally prone to root rot but you still need to maintain medium moisture. I wouldn't use straight soil, but mixing it with some perlite and sphagnum moss would be ideal. Place the wet stick on top and cover the container to give the cutting more humidity to work with. Remember to poke a few holes in the plastic covering for sufficient air circulation, and place the container in a bright, warm place. In a few months, the cutting should root and hopefully a new baby leaf will pop up!

2. Philodendron White Princess

Philodendron White Princess is a stunning houseplant that has gained popularity in recent years. It is a variegated philodendron, with dark green leaves that have creamy white stripes and speckles. The leaves of the White Princess tend to be smaller than those of other philodendron varieties (as we'll get into soon), but they are still large enough to make a statement in any room.

Propagating Philodendron White Princess can be done through stem cuttings following the same care instructions as the monstera thai constellation, fiddle-leaf fig tree, etc.

Philodendron White Princess can also be propagated through division, which involves separating the plant into smaller sections and planting them into individual pots — as we've covered several times for other plants earlier.

3. Philodendron Melanochrysum

Philodendron Melanochrysum is a popular tropical plant that has large, velvety green leaves with prominent veins. The leaves of this plant can grow up to two feet long, making it an impressive and striking houseplant.

Propagation of Philodendron Melanochrysum is commonly done through stem cuttings. For this plant specifically, it's essential to frequently mist the leaves regularly to maintain a sufficiently high humidity level. Also create a mini greenhouse effect by covering the pot with some plastic wrap!

Propagation can also be done through division, but it is a bit more challenging because of the plant's unique growth pattern. Divide the plant only when it has multiple stems or crowns growing from the same base and then follow the same procedure as you've learnt for other plants (e.g. moth orchids).

4. Philodendron Gloriosum

Philodendron Gloriosum is another popular tropical plant that has big, heart-shaped leaves with a velvety texture and striking vein patterns. Propagating Philodendron Gloriosum can be done through stem cuttings, which is a relatively easy process.

Start by finding a healthy, long stem of about three to six inches in length. Make sure it has some leaves and roots attached and cut the stem at the point where it meets the main crown, being careful not to damage the main stem. Put the stem in a fresh pot of soil somewhere with indirect sunlight and water it. Wait a few weeks and you should have a brand new Gloriosum!

5. Anthurium Veitchii

If you're a fan of large foliage in houseplants, the Anthurium Veitchii won't leave you asking for more. It's got surprisingly huge leaves that are thick and glossy. It'll instantly steal the spotlight in your entire display of houseplants which earns it a well-deserved nickname of "The King" — not to be confused with The Queen (Anthurium Warocqueanum) which is covered next.

You can propagate this stunner in several ways, but stem cuttings and division are the two most popular ones.

Steps for Division

1. Gently remove the mother plant from its pot and carefully separate the roots into two or more sections.
2. Each section should have at least one stem and healthy roots.
3. Plant section(s) in a separate pot with well-draining soil and water thoroughly.

Steps for Propagation Through Stem Cuttings

1. Choose a healthy stem with several leaves attached.
2. Cut the stem just below a node (where a leaf attaches to the stem) using a clean, sharp knife or scissors.

3. Remove the bottom leaves and dip the cut end into rooting hormone (optional).
4. Plant the cutting in a pot with moist potting soil and keep it in a warm, humid location with bright, indirect light.
5. Water the cutting regularly and mist the leaves to keep them from drying out.

6. Anthurium Warocqueanum

The Anthurium Warocqueanum has a striking beauty that very few houseplants can match. The shape of its leaves effortlessly stands out since it's unlike any other. The leaves can even get up to 4 feet in length, so you can only imagine how majestic it'd look.

The plant is a bit challenging when it comes to maintenance, though. Since it's picky about its water, light, and temperature requirements, it might not be the right pickup for a beginner. But if you've already got one and it's thriving, why not multiply it for free?

The main way to propagate the Queen Anthurium is to snip a cutting of a shot that's newly growing from the main stem. You can separate it and grow it as a fresh new plant, but you'll have to time it right. Cutting any new offshoots too early will not only have low chances of successful propagation, but can also be detrimental to the mother plant's health.

7. Monstera obliqua Peruvian Form

Ooh, here's a personal favorite. Just a glance at this plant will make you want it right away! If you've got a thing for exotic-looking plants, of course. The Monstera obliqua Peruvian Form is a super rare, highly coveted variety of Monstera, known for its unusual-looking leaves with large, oval-shaped holes. It is a climbing plant native to the tropical rainforests of South and Central America and is considered one of the most difficult plants to cultivate due to its very particular requirements for growth and propagation.

It can be propagated through stem cuttings, using either water or soil as the rooting medium. For the best shot at success, always take your cuttings during the growing season (spring to summer). Make sure your cutting has at least one node and leaf attached as rooting won't occur without it! Then, stick it in a new pot using a loam & peat compost mixture and water the top layer generously. Keep it sufficiently moist throughout the rooting period and you should start to see some development in just a few weeks. Once a healthy amount of roots form and strengthen, feel free to pot it into a separate pot with a fresh mix!

8. Philodendron Pink Princess

The Philodendron Pink Princess — as you can probably guess by the name — is a breathtaking hybrid plant. It's known for its variegated foliage which ranges in color from dark green to pink and white. Being a tropical plant, it's native to the rainforests of Central and South America and is a popular choice among houseplant enthusiasts due to its unique colors.

You can propagate this plant through stem cuttings. Snip a stem from about a quarter of an inch away below the node, making sure there are at least some pink-ish leaves attached. Feel free to take more than one cutting for better chances of success. Place the stems into water in a way that the node gets fully submerged but not the leaves. Pick a warm spot with plenty of indirect sunlight for them. Root systems should form after a month! Wait until they're about two inches long and then report on arid soil mix.

You could also propagate this plant by division. Carefully lift the root ball out of the pot and gently comb the soil away. With the root system exposed, look to find baby plants with a developed root system and step. Separate them and repot them as individual little plants, following the same care instructions as above.

9. Variegated Syngonium

The Variegated Syngonium isn't the fanciest looking plant out there unlike some of the other species we've covered in this list, but its variegated leaves and ease of propagation make it a worthy mention. It's a vining plant that's extremely easy to grow and multiply! In fact, folks living in tropical areas will actually have to restrict it to a pot so that it doesn't spread on its own.

The simplest method to propagate this plant is through stem cuttings. In spring or summer, select healthy stems having at least one leaf and three nodes. The rooting medium can either be moist soil or a jar of water as long as you place it in a humid, warm, and well-lit (without direct sun exposure). The plants should be ready to pot within a month!

FINAL TAKEAWAY

In the last two chapters, we've learnt all about the ins and out of plant propagation. In this particular one, we went over carefully curated lists of plants to try and propagate based on your level of experience. We also covered step-by-step guides and tips describing exactly what you need to do to multiply each plant.

So far, we've only talked about the beauty, benefits, and wonders of houseplants. But the next chapter covers quite the opposite! In chapter 6, you'll learn how some houseplants are actually **toxic**, despite their friendly and attractive looks! So keep reading to find out which ones you need to be careful with to avoid harming yourself or your loved ones...

6

TOXIC INDOOR PLANTS

I n earlier chapters, we've gone over the many life-changing benefits that plants can have on our well-being. It can not only improve our respiratory well-being, but also our mental health by alleviating stress symptoms. But, there's another side to plants as well. Did you know that some of them can be toxic?

Toxicity in plants comes from many different chemical toxins like glycosides, amino acids, proteins, and alkaloids. Not all species have the same type of sensitivity or reaction to intoxication from these plants. Since some houseplants can also be toxic, humans (especially children) and common house pets like cats and dogs can often be exposed to these effects.

This chapter looks at a list of poisonous houseplants to tell you which plants you should be wary of. Don't worry, toxicity in houseplants doesn't have to be a complete deal-breaker, but there are just a few safety tips that you need to keep in mind to keep yourself and your loved ones safe. So without further ado, let's get into it.

POISONOUS HOUSEPLANTS

1. Dumb Cane

Dumb Cane (Dieffenbachia) is a tropical plant that requires very little light as it's used to being in the shade of large trees in its natural habitat. Interestingly enough, the plant's name comes from the effects that you may experience upon ingesting it. Its sap can cause a burning sensation and swelling of the tongue. The swelling not only makes you temporarily "dumb" (or "mute" as some people like to say), but can even block air off to the throat, making it potentially fatal to both pets and humans.

But with that said, the plant's beautiful nonetheless, and the risk of ingesting it accidentally can be easily avoided with a plant stand.

Use one to keep it well out of reach of small dogs, cats, or toddlers.

2. English Ivy

We've talked about this one before, and yes, it's also toxic. Serious problems can be caused if someone were to ingest it in large quantities, causing symptoms like burning throat, skin irritation, rashes, and fever. Since the plant naturally tends to trail, you can set it somewhere high off the ground to keep it away from pets and children.

3. Easter Lily

Easter lilies not only have gorgeous white blooms, but also a lovely scent that'll have you saving money on room fresheners. Beautiful as they are, they aren't the safest plants out there if you're a cat person. Even small amounts of any part of this plant can potentially prove to be life-threatening for your cat upon ingestion. Failure to get appropriate treatment within the next 18 hours can lead to kidney failure.

Not only that, pollen itself is toxic to felines, so make sure to keep the plant outside of your cat's access, and remember to actively get rid of yellow stamens in the blooming season. Luckily, the plant isn't poisonous to children.

4. Peace Lily

Here's another plant we've already talked about, and you guessed it, it's toxic too — but only if its leaves are eaten in a large quantity. If you've got young ones or pets in your home, this plant is best enjoyed at a distance. Pick a spot that's well out of their reach. No matter where you put it though, the deep green foliage will still have its presence felt in the room.

5. Daffodils

Love the blooming season but can't wait for it? Well, forcing bulbs indoors is always an option. It basically means creating favorable conditions for a plant to bloom flowers outside of its natural spring season. But doing so with some spring bulbs (like daffodils and hyacinths) can prove to be toxic upon ingestion by pets and humans. It's easy to mistake the bulbs for onions or shallots, and it could potentially prove lethal. In most cases, though, patients only experience symptoms like high blood pressure or irregular heartbeat temporarily.

Those symptoms are still extremely dangerous, so make sure to keep your daffodils in a spot they can't be tampered with. The safer route is to grow them in a terrarium to keep them away from your loved ones altogether.

6. Philodendron

Philodendrons are one of the most popular groups of indoor plants out there, but they're not completely safe for us or our furry friends. If you were to eat them by accident, you'd be at risk of swelling and a burning sensation in your throat, tongue, and lips. Not scary enough? Add vomiting and diarrhea to the mix and you'd know not to keep it in reach of your toddler or pet.

7. Pothos

No matter how harmless the Pothos plant looks, it shares the same symptoms as the philodendron upon ingestion. If that's not enough to keep you from buying this plant (which is totally understandable), I'd recommend potting it in a hanging basket for extra safety.

8. Sago Palm

If you're a fan of tropical plants in your home, the Sago Palm could be a must-have! It's a miniature palm that effortlessly creates forest-y vibes. It's actually one of the oldest species of plants on the planet, and that's partially because animals know not to eat it. The entire plant (including its roots and seeds) is poisonous. Aside from symptoms like vomiting and diarrhea, it can even cause death by liver failure. If you plan on having one of these in your home, choose a spot that makes it completely inaccessible for your little ones!

9. ZZ Plant

The ZZ is one of the easiest plants to look after since it's so drought-tolerant and hard to kill. It can easily light up any room be it your bedroom or a gloomy office cabin. But, much like the Sago Palm, all parts of the ZZ plant are also toxic. Aside from the risk of ingestion, you should also wash your hands/gloves after having handled the plant. Fortunately, you don't have to touch it that often since the plant doesn't require too much care to live or thrive in an indoor setting.

SAFETY TIPS FOR TOXIC PLANTS

We've gone over some of the most common houseplants that aren't as harmless as they may seem, but what should you do about it?

While the thought of your child ingesting any part of these poisonous plants is horrific, it's luckily very simple to keep that from happening. Here are a few safety tips that can help prevent that.

- **Make toxic plants inaccessible to children** by placing them in specific rooms where your pets or children may not be allowed. You can also use hard-to-reach spots like the top of a bookshelf or a cupboard to make sure your kid or dog can't get close.
- **Use labeling** to highlight whether or not a plant is toxic. If you've got a child that's old enough to read or learn cues, you can tell them which plants they need to be careful with. For instance, plants with a red label on them should never be touched or eaten, while plants with a green label are safe to feel or interact with.
- **Be careful while discarding clippings.** Even poisonous plants need occasional pruning, so firstly, use gloves when you do that. Secondly, think about where you'll put the clippings. The trash can isn't the safest outlet for them since pets and toddlers topple them over all the time, which could lead to ingestion if they get curious.
- **Fertilizers and potting soils should also be out of reach.** Aside from toxic plants, some of the products

used in their upkeep can also have harmful chemicals and they're not safe for human ingestion either. So if you have kids at home, be sure to tightly shut the lids on your fertilizers and potting soils and store them well away from the reach of your children/pets.

- **Checfi for mildew and mold regularly.** Even plants that are not toxic by nature can become dangerous if they're inflicted by mold and mildew. So check your soil and pots for signs frequently to take corrective measures on a timely basis since it's a potential health hazard for the whole family.

- **Retire cracked/broken pots.** Another fairly common risk factor that often goes under the radar in many homes are damaged pots. Plant pots that are cracked or broken offer favorable conditions for moisture to accumulate, which in turn attracts pests and promotes mold growth. This not only deteriorates the plant's health, but also makes it dangerous for the surrounding environment. So keep an eye out for cracks in your pots and replace them as soon as possible!

- **Hanging baskets can also be dangerous.** Hanging toxic plants from the ceiling is one of the safest ways to keep it completely out of reach of pets and children, but it creates an all-new risk factor as well. If the basket isn't sturdy enough to hold the weight of a large plant, it could quite literally break off and give you (or one of your family members) head trauma. So if you're gonna use hanging pots, make sure they're well-built and designed to hold hefty plants safely. It goes without saying, also make sure your ceiling hooks and plant shelves are also sturdy enough to hold the weight of the houseplant in question.

- **Think twice about the positioning of vining plants.** As we've learnt from the list before, there are quite a few vining plants that are poisonous. Even if you place one of these on top of a shelf, some of its tendrils can grow long enough for your child to tug it off.
- **Ensure fresh water availability for pets at all times.** If you forget to refill your pet's water container, they can sometimes be tempted to drink from your plant's tray. This can also be super dangerous since toxins from poisonous plants can leach into the water.
- **Always have an emergency plan!** Take as many preventative measures as you can, but make sure you always have an emergency plan in case things somehow do go south. Speaking of which...

WHAT TO DO WHEN PET HAS EATEN A POISONOUS HOUSEPLANT

As soon as you find out that your pet has ingested a poisonous houseplant, the first step is to stay calm. Not all houseplants are toxic, and even the ones that are typically don't prove to be fatal unless your pet eats a very *large* quantity. In most cases, the worst-case scenario is a temporarily unwell pet.

Your move is to look for common symptoms of houseplant poisoning in your pet like vomiting, drooling, diarrhea, disorientation, and confusion. Then, try to find out the quantity and type of plant that your pet has ingested. Give your vet a call immediately and share as much relevant information as you can, and then do as advised.

WHAT TO DO WHEN A CHILD HAS EATEN A POISONOUS HOUSEPLANT

Children are naturally curious, and parents love that. But, in the case of toxic houseplants, this natural instinct can prove to be super dangerous. If you're a parent to both, a child and a poisonous houseplant, it's wise to always be prepared for the worst-case scenario!

Toddlers and babies have a habit of taking everything in their mouth, which is why they can also sometimes play with or eat parts of houseplants. Luckily, the rate of casualties occurring from these incidents is very low, so once again, remember to be as calm as possible if you encounter such a situation.

First, find out what your child has eaten and how much of it. To avoid confusion, try to identify the Latin name since many plants with subtle differences tend to share the same non-Latin names. Immediately get into contact with a hospital, local general physician, or any healthcare provider for professional advice.

Hopefully, you'll never have to use any of the above information in the future, but it's imperative to always have it at the back of your mind in case of emergencies.

This chapter was all about looking after your family and pets against the potential dangers of toxic plants. We've gone over a number of preventive and corrective measures you can take to do just that. But plants are family too! So, the next couple of chapters are all about equipping you with specialized tips to take excellent care of them.

We'll be looking at some golden advice for looking after delicate plant types like low-light ones and succulents.

The information shared in these upcoming chapters is essential for making you a badass plant parent that can handle even the toughest situations well. But there's a lot to unpack in that department, so keep reading!

7

TIPS FOR SUCCULENTS

S ucculents have been on fire for quite some time within the houseplant trends, and they deserve every bit of the spotlight they're getting. Whether you're a minimalist or just like things that are chic and cute, it's almost impossible to go wrong with a succulent pickup. They originate from dry, desert-esque locations, and their name comes from their sap-filled, thick leaves (deriving from the Latin word "sucus" meaning sap).

Unlike most other plant families, succulents aren't just limited to the color green. In fact, you can find a succulent in just about any shade of the rainbow so feel free to take your pick! Now, by this description, it's easy to also start thinking of cacti — and you'd be kinda right. That's because all cacti are succulents, but not all succulents are cacti. A cactus has spines or thorns along its stem but succulents don't necessarily have to be that mean-looking.

If all this succulent talk makes you want to grab an agave or stonecrop plant right away, you'll want to know what's coming ahead in this chapter. We'll discuss some precious tips to help you look after them well, as well as some exciting DIY projects you can work on with them. Let's get into it!

WHAT ARE SOME COMMON SUCCULENTS?

Bringing a succulent home is a fun way of introducing some character into your already impressive collection of house-plants. But with over 10,000 different types of succulents, picking one or two isn't the easiest decision to make. We don't even know how many varieties are out there since the term "succulent" is pretty wide, and can even be attributed to any plant that's evolved to survive and adapt in arid conditions. It's apparently a term defining a certain quality of a plant rather than a plant family or species. In fact, experts say that a plant can even become more or less succulent according to the changes they experience in their climate conditions. In that sense, the word is more of an adjective than a noun, with the number of varieties not even being fixed or quantifiable.

But with that said, all succulents do still have quite a lot of common ground between them. They all hail from dry or hot climates and don't require much watering at all to thrive. In one way or another, all succulents have evolved to have a certain physical characteristic that allows them to retain moisture effectively to be able to go for long periods without another watering. It could be anything between thick stems or rhizomes to plump leaves.

I'll leave you with a list of 17 of my favorite succulents to help narrow down the search for you. They're all super easy to care for and can easily live on occasional waterings, so feel free to go with any plant that looks like the right match for you.

★ Haworthia
★ Aloe
★ Echeveria
★ Jade Plant
★ Snake Plant
★ ZZ Plant
★ String of Pearls
★ Hoya
★ Sempervivum
★ Peperomia
★ Kalanchoe
★ Dracaena
★ Gasteria
★ Euphorbia
★ Agave
★ Ice Plant
★ Moonstone Plant

TIPS FOR SUCCULENTS

1. Start with the right potting mix

You can easily find potting soil mixtures that are especially made for succulents. Unlike regular potting mix, soil for succulents doesn't aim to retain more moisture with a high volume of organic matter.

For succulents, you need a mix that's well-draining since these plants are sensitive to overwatering. You could even make a simple DIY mix for succulents with some sand and perlite and should work just fine.

You'll get different answers on "the right soil for succulents" no matter how many people you ask. But they'll probably have something to help retain a little bit of fertilizer and moisture, while still allowing excess water to quickly drain away.

Now, that's just my general recommendation for succulents, but as you know there are 10,000 varieties of these plants. Since it's impossible to get into specifics, it's best to check the soil requirements for your particular succulent plant and find what works best for it.

2. Make Sure Your Planter Has Sufficient Drainage Holes

From fancy-looking (and not to mention, expensive) plant pots to a DIY solution made with cinder blocks, you can plant succulents in just about anything if you know what you're doing. Whichever route you go through, always make sure the planter has one or more drainage holes to avoid water logging the plant. This advice applies to almost all plants out there, but since succulents are extremely sensitive to overwatering, it deserves a special mention here.

I'd also suggest steering clear of plastic-based DIY options when you're creating a planter for succulents. That's because water doesn't evaporate as quickly in plastic pots which could become a risk factor for root rot in succulents, so you're better off using terra-cotta or ceramic pots since they're breathable.

We've planted succulents in pretty much everything imaginable — cinder blocks, thrift store bowls, hollowed-out books — the sky's really the limit once you get the hang of caring for them. However, try to always make sure your planter has a drainage hole.

Succulents should never sit in standing water; it quickly leads to root rot, so proper drainage is essential.

3. Go Easy on the Water

If you pay attention, there's a bit of a theme going on here. Water's the villain to look out for with succulents. That's weird to say because they really can't survive without it, but the phrase "less is more" really holds true with this family of plants. You don't have to water succulents frequently unlike most other houseplants.

If you're not used to caring for succulents, it's advisable to stick to the most reliable way of watering them. What's that, you might ask? Well, just fill a saucer with water and place your planter in it. The water will start to get absorbed into the soil through the drainage holes down under. Once it finishes up or stops decreasing, put the planter back to its spot. Ta-da!

4. Don't Ignore Them

Just because someone's tough and resilient doesn't mean they don't need love! Same goes for succulents. Since they're naturally some of the lowest-maintenance plants out there, it's easy to unconsciously start ignoring them. That's a deadly mistake!

Even if you don't have to water or prune them as much, you've still gotta check them regularly for spider mites, aphids, or mealy bugs. These pests will feast on your succulent and if left unchecked, could even end up killing the poor thing!

5. Keep Them Comfortably Warm

While cacti are excellent at handling extremely hot temperatures, not all succulents have that resilience. Most thrive in temperatures between the range of 70 to 90 degrees Fahrenheit. You can put them near a window indoors, or in the shade outside. Freezing temperatures will almost certainly prove to be lethal for succulents, so if you live somewhere with a cold climate, they'll have to be kept exclusively indoors.

6. Get the Light Right

For succulents, a fifty-fifty split between shade and sunlight works best. Leaving them in full sun all day can burn the leaves, while too little of it can lead to frailness. But since that too is a spectrum for these 10,000 varieties, here's a quick rule of thumb to go by for you. If they're spiky, they'll need more sun — if they're variegated, yellow, or green, they like shade.

If you plan to keep your succulents outside, a spot that gets sunlight in the morning and then shade in the afternoon would be ideal. Indoors, however, a south-facing window should be just fine.

7. Give Them Sun To Keep Em' Vibrant

Succulent plants that are colorful will need about 6 hours of sun a day to maintain those rich shades and bright hues. A lack of sunlight can cause them to go back to their "greenness" and elongate. It's not necessarily a problem, but they just won't look as impressive as they can. The deepest hues will come out in the outer ranges of cold and hot temperatures. So, they'll naturally come in during the spring season when they get sunny days and chilly nights!

8. Let Them Sleep During Winter

Succulents grow mostly in the summer, and often go dormant in winters. When it gets cold, they rest and wait for spring and summer to step on the gas with growth. In the winter, it's best not to give them any fertilizer. Also, water them just enough to keep the pot from fully drying out. In their dormant days, their already-high root rot risks get even worse, so you'll have to make some adjustments to your watering schedule in the winter. And don't worry, the nutrients and water retained in their leaves will be more than enough to keep them going until spring arrives!

9. Take Them Outside

Keeping succulents exclusively indoors isn't the best for them (unless of course, it's freezing cold outside). Give them a chance to enjoy a bit of a vacation in the spring and summer days. Let some rain hit them with all its unique minerals that you won't find in tap water. The fresh air circulation won't hurt too! But still, be careful not to put them in direct sunlight as that can easily burn the leaves on some varieties.

10. Feed Them

Succulents grow like crazy in spring and summer. So much so that they'll even make up for all that dormancy in the winter. This is when you need to feed your plant with all the delicious nutrients it needs to take full advantage of this growing season. My general recommendation for most succulents would be a high-quality 10-10-10 fertilizer that's half-strength diluted.

PROPAGATING SUCCULENTS

We've already gone over the steps, tips, and hacks for propagating many different plant varieties. But since this chapter is dedicated to succulents, here are the specialized steps you should follow to propagate them well!

Luckily, these guys are some of the easiest ones to propagate. In fact, if you've had them for long enough, you'd know that some of these can even multiply on their own without you trying. Leaves can fall off on the soil which can initiate a new baby plant in the right conditions, without any involvement on your part!

The simplest steps to do it are as follows:

1. Use a sharp, clean pair of scissors to carefully cut one or more healthy succulent leaves. It's important to cut it right from the stem to get the whole leaf because the cutting may not root without it. Also, try not to cut too many leaves off the mother plant as that potentially puts it at risk.
2. Let your cuttings air dry for a couple days and then place them on top of a container filled with some succulent mix with good drainage.
3. Next, all you've gotta do is wait. It could take several weeks before the roots start sprouting out. Once that happens, just water it sparingly and soon enough, you should see some cute little succulents starting to form!

DIY PROJECTS

Succulents are a treat to have for folks who like doing some DIY work for their houseplants. They'll give you plenty of opportunities to get creative with them. Here are two of my favorite projects that I'd definitely suggest you try with your succulents!

1. Succulents in Containers

Here's everything you'll need for this!

Tools

1. A brush with soft bristles
2. Sharp and clean scissors

Materials

1. Succulent plants (I know, obvious)
2. Some landscape fabric
3. Potting mix for succulents or cacti (whichever applies)
4. Cool-looking decorative items like marbles, gravel, glass, or stones
5. A planter with drainage holes

Here's What To Do

- **Hole coverage**

Grab your plastic screening and cut a piece that's large enough to cover all the drainage holes in your container. This makes sure the soil doesn't leak out while still letting all the excess moisture out.

- **Potting mix**

Use enough potting mix to make sure the soil line remains about half an inch below the container's rim after putting your succulents in place. Having at least this much margin makes it easier for you to water your plants without making an over-flowing mess.

- **Testing**

Now you've got to test it out. With your plants still in the nursery pots they came in, place them into the container to see how much space they need. Move them around until you're happy with the arrangement.

- **Plant the container**

Now we're talking business. It's time to dislocate your plants out of the nursery pots and gently put them into the container(s) you've prepared (see tip below). Carefully pack on some extra potting mix around the succulents until the soil is at the same level as it was in the nursery pot (relative to the plants).

Be sure to fill in all the spaces between your plants as air gaps can lead to excess dryness for the roots, which could be fatal for your plants.

Tip: Not every nursery pot is thoughtfully prepared to make dislocation easy for you. The best way to get your plants out safely is to hold the plant gently from the top, keeping its stem between your thumb and index finger. Then, turn the pot sideways and tap its bottom to ease the plant out.

- **Be wary of overcrowding**

Also, make sure you leave enough space between plants as overcrowding can lead to slower growth and unhealthy plants as they compete for nutrients and water. Similarly, light and air may also not freely reach every plant in a tight container so if you've got several plants — feel free to use larger or multiple pots to give them all sufficient space to thrive in.

- **Final touch ups**

Now that your brand new baby succulents are all set and happy in their new homes, all that's left to do are some finishing touches. By that, I mean getting rid of the soil that may be covering the plants' leaves and/or stems. A soft-bristle brush works best for this part. If you don't have one, simply blowing on them can also get most of the job done.

With that out of the way, you can earn some brownie points by adding a top dressing of aesthetic-looking coarse materials like glass, marbles, gravel, or stones. You can go with neutral shades or bright hues depending on the type of look you're after.

2. An Indoor Succulent Garden

Here's another exciting DIY venture for those of you looking to grow your succulents outdoors. Remember, you can only do this if you live somewhere with a climate that's favorable for succulents. It's not a good idea for northern parts of the world where it's mostly cold throughout the year.

If that caveat doesn't apply to you, I'd certainly recommend trying this one out for yourself! Also, I'd suggest doing this with cacti exclusively because many succulents cannot stand being in the sun all day long, but cacti (the ones having spikes along the stem) tend to have excellent resilience against that.

Here's what you need

1. A bowl with a wide mouth
2. Appropriate potting mix
3. Potting mix for cacti (if you're on a budget, you can DIY this too using ingredients like sand to make the mix more porous)
4. A variety of cacti with various shapes, textures, or even colors
5. Some gravel
6. Light and water

Here's what to do

1. At the bottom of your wide-mouth bowl, place a layer of gravel that's about two inches thick. This allows excellent drainage which is vital since succulents are so susceptible to root rot.
2. Lay your cactus potting mix on top. The soil should have superb drainage with minimal water retention.
3. Get planting! Starting with the biggest succulent in your batch, remove it from its pot in the same way as suggested in the tip above. I'd suggest wearing gloves for this one because these types of plants have sharp edges and thorns and they can easily hurt you.
4. Plan your placement in a way that peppers the colors of your succulent variety around. You don't have to worry about overcrowding here so don't worry about planting your cacti too close. The closer they are, the lusher your arrangement will seem. Since these plants will be out in the open, there's going to be enough light and air to go around for all of them. As for water, they need as little of it as possible anyway!
5. Make sure you completely cover all the roots with soil. Add it wherever it's needed to envelop each plant's roots well.
6. Now it's time to finally take it outside! If you've got a misting setting on your water hose, use it to give your soil some initial moisture to work with. If you don't have a misting hose, you can simply use a spray bottle. Water sparingly though!

FINAL TAKEAWAY

This chapter must have been a treat for succulent lovers! I for one, am someone whose houseplant collection can't be complete without having some succulents around to spice things up. Living in Miami's rainy, humid climate though, I always need to grow my

succulents in containers indoors to be better able to control their soil and irrigation. But no matter where you live, the information shared in this chapter should be more than enough to keep you covered in all situations.

Succulents, fortunately, are some of the easiest plants to care for. On the other hand, we have plants that are super picky about their environment and need some extra care and love to thrive in your home. One such example is low-light plants, and that's what the next chapter is all about. So, keep on reading!

8

CARING FOR LOW-LIGHT PLANTS

E veryone knows that cacti need a lot of daylight to thrive as they're used to the hot, sunny climate of the desert. On the other end of that spectrum, we also have plants that are the exact opposite of that. Too much direct light can easily prove problematic, and even fatal to them. In layman's terms, they're categorized as "low-light indoor plants" and they'll happily decorate every corner of your room without ever having to face a window!

In this chapter, we're taking a deep dive into the specifics of this unique category of plants. You'll learn about a variety of promising low-light houseplants and some specialized care tips to better understand their needs. Let's begin!

BEST LOW-LIGHT INDOOR PLANTS

1. Lucky Bamboo

First up, we have the lucky bamboo plant. You could grow this one in either soil or water media and they work well in both, home and office settings. They have a pretty distinct look with their sculptural, bamboo-shaped stalks patterned with tiny green leaves. If you like having houseplants that have some personality and don't just look like "every other plant" — lucky bamboo might be the one for you.

The plant is super hard to kill so it's also very beginner-friendly. It can thrive on very little light and can do very well in full-shade spots. Just keep them away from pets though because they do have some toxicity, the risks of which we've already discussed in chapter 6. You should also make sure the plant isn't exposed to any cold or warm drafts in your home!

2. Spider Plant

The spider plant is known for being a super easy plant all-round. It's easy to grow and naturally adapts well to many different types of environments. The name comes from its flowers that are star-shaped, and evolve into green offshoots that resemble a spider.

You can grow these as trailing or hanging plants, and you won't even have to worry about opening your curtains for them because they can survive for a long time without getting much daylight. As long as you water the plant regularly to keep the soil from drying out, the plant should be just fine!

3. Golden Pothos

The Golden Pothos is another resilient plant species that can thrive in very tough conditions. Aside from extremely low-light spots, it can even survive through a period of near-complete lack of water. That's rare for a non-succulent plant but the golden pothos pull it off easily.

Thanks to its ease of growing, hardiness, and those gorgeous heart-shaped, leathery smooth leaves, it's one of the most popular species among houseplant enthusiasts around the world. Just be careful not to let pests feast on your plants, and occasionally loosen and dust your golden pothos vines to keep them from getting tangled.

4. Snake Plant

Next we have Sansevieria. Not only does this plant require very little light indoors, but also very little care and maintenance! It's a complete stunner with its thick, sword-shaped leaves and vertical growth that can reach heights of up to 8 feet.

The snake plant is especially long-lived with healthy and well-kept ones thriving for decades on end. Ideally, it grows best in partial shade, but doesn't necessarily need it to thrive. It tolerates shady conditions very well as long as you don't overwater the plant (since there's not gonna be any sun to evaporate it away any time soon).

5. Staghorn Fern

Next, we have an epiphytic plant called Staghorn ferns. The term "epiphytic" means that these ferns can naturally grow on other plants instead of soil. The leaves on these plants have a bright green shade and can grow large. Since they somewhat resemble the shape of deer antlers, the name "staghorn" is quite fitting.

These plants are fairly sensitive and can actually burn in direct sunlight, which is why shade spots are their comfort zone! Keep in mind that these plants aren't easy to look after by any means, so only get your hands on one if you're experienced and looking for a challenge!

6. English Ivy

English Ivy is a highly versatile plant when it comes to its light preferences. It can be grown both indoors and outdoors. From giving an appealing trailing effect with its delicate leaves indoors, to being spread out as a ground cover outdoors, the choice is all yours. For the indoor option, pick a spot in your home that receives at least some indirect light during the day. Maintain a sufficient amount of humidity for the plant by misting it regularly. At night, it prefers a relatively cool room to rest peacefully, but keep the plant away from drafts!

As you already know from chapter 6, this plant is toxic! So make sure you also place it in a way that makes it inaccessible for your pets and children (if any).

7. Cast Iron Plant

As you can probably guess by the name, cast iron plants are nearly indestructible. Everything about them is rugged and hardy, which makes the adjective "handsome" more suitable than "beautiful" if you'd ask me.

They have large, arching glossy leaves in a deep green color. From a lack of water to receiving very little light throughout the day, this plant can stick it out through all sorts of neglect. Ideally, though, they should be watered when the top layer of the soil becomes dry. Put them near a north-facing window since they only need indirect light as being exposed to the sun can burn the leaves.

8. Peace Lily

Peace lilies are popular houseplants and they're great at being domesticated. Since the plant is naturally shade-loving, being under a roof is actually good for it. Like the cast iron plant, peace lilies too can withstand some neglect on your part. They will, however, need to be hydrated to make sure their foliage doesn't start to wilt.

9. Maidenhair Fern

I love the shape of the cute little leaves on the Maidenhair Fern! The clustered foliage paired with its dark stems create a captivating look despite the plant being pretty small, so put them wherever you want to add a little pop of green around the house.

These ferns need to always have moisture (but not sogginess) in their soil to thrive, so be sure to regularly water them. They do best in slightly warmer temperatures and sufficient humidity with indirect light.

10. ZZ Plant

Yep, we have yet another mention of this regular customer — the ZZ Plant. One reason behind its sky-high popularity among houseplant enthusiasts is its ability to thrive with little to no natural sunlight. From windowless offices to home basements, the ZZ plant is always a promising solution to bring a pop of nature to your abode. Ideally, though, the plant should be placed in a spot that gets lots of indirect daylight but no direct sun.

11. Philodendron

With easily manageable care requirements, the philodendrons offer a simple way to introduce a jungle-like aesthetic to your urban home. The plant has long, green vines which will regularly need to be dusted to be always at their best, but it's all worth it. The ideal spot for these plants would be a window receiving bright but indirect sunlight.

12. Anthurium

Ah, the Anthurium. Just taking a glance at this plant in its bloom could be enough to make your day. It has lush foliage throughout the year and bright flowers during the spring and summer seasons. You can grow these indoors with some way to bump the humidity up a notch around them (unless the environment is naturally humid where you live). The soil also needs to be consistently moist but not soggy. Direct sun can burn the Anthurium's leaves, so it's best kept in bright but indirect light during the day. Since this plant is also toxic, be sure to keep it well away from pets and children.

13. Chinese Evergreen

The Chinese Evergreen is an excellent indoor low-light plant as it thrives in partial to full shade. Direct sunlight exposure can burn the leaves pretty easily on this one, so be extra careful when you pick a spot for it! Its leaves are glossy green and grow in an oval shape on short stems. Warning: this plant is toxic too! So, keep it out of range of your little ones and pets.

14. Swiss Cheese Plant

Love the look of large, leathery green leaves around the house? The swiss cheese plant is the one you're looking for. It's also called the split-leaf philodendron and it naturally grows well in shady spots.

Pick a location that gets a lot of indirect light indoors, but no direct sun at all. Too much exposure to bright light could be enough to burn the foliage! If you've got some furry friends running around the house, you might want to place this at the top of your bookshelf since it's toxic to pets.

15. Prayer Plant

Lastly, we have the prayer plant. With tricolor leaves and an awesome-looking pattern on it, it's my go-to plant to add a touch of character anywhere you want around the house. From your work desk to the center table in your living room, this little tropical plant is the perfect choice to boost the aesthetics! Like most other plants on this list, direct sunlight can burn the foliage of the prayer plant and it has a pretty high tolerance of low-light conditions. A location that gets bright but indirect light works best!

CARING FOR LOW-LIGHT PLANTS

Don't get a lot of sunny days where you live? Don't have enough window space in your home to fulfill your desire of having loads of houseplants? Worry not, the world of plants is diverse, and there's always something for everyone. In your case, you can take your pick from any of the 15 lovely plant species listed above (and many more). Here are a few key tips to help you take good care of them!

- Remember to turn your low-light plants regularly. Even though they don't need a lot of light to thrive, they still need an even amount of it on all sides to avoid nutritional imbalances and asymmetric growth.
- If the conditions discussed above apply to you, always be careful with your choices when you're in the nursery to pick up new plants. If you don't get much sun, for instance, getting a cactus isn't the right move. You need hardy plants like the philodendron, cast iron, pothos, sansevieria, and Chinese evergreens as they don't care much about lack of light.
- Even if you can't give your plants an abundance of indirect light to work with, you should still try to help them secure as much of it as possible. Find the brightest spots available inside your home for them and try to occasionally rotate them from higher to lower lit areas for best results. Moving plants regularly encourages them to capture the light they need to sustain healthy growth consistently.
- Low-light indoor plants typically don't need a lot of water to thrive. In fact, it's easy to go overboard with watering these species. Only give them a drink when it's needed (stick a finger about an inch into their soil to see if it's dry), but feel free to water thoroughly. Remember to pour off the water that remains at the top of the pot after the plant absorbs what it needs!
- You don't have to fertilize these plants either! At least not the ones that aren't actively growing. Only use it sparingly for plants that you'd like to give a nutritional boost to stimulate faster growth.

- Some indoor plants may not be able to survive in the sun, but they can still need a fair amount of light to thrive and grow at an ideal rate. If the conditions in your home aren't ideal for providing bright yet indirect light, consider supplementing your plant with some additional artificial lighting (red for flowering plants and blue for foliage).
- Since these plants won't be getting any direct sun to evaporate away the excess water content, they're a bit more susceptible to root rot. To avoid this, make sure you use airy soil that makes use of better ventilation to dry out unneeded moisture. Perlite and pumice, for instance, would be the ideal ingredients in your soil mix.
- Despite these plants being categorized as "low-light", there's always something such as "too low" light. That's why you've got to know the signs to look for if your plants can't get much light in your home. Leggy growth is one, for instance, where the plant starts to stretch and reach for light sources to sustain itself. Stunted growth, excessive leaf dropping, leaf discoloration, and a failure to bloom are a few other symptoms that are self-explanatory! If you notice any of these, it means it's either time to find a brighter spot, or to supplement your plant's light intake through artificial LEDs.

FINAL TAKEAWAY

Having read this chapter, you no longer have to feel left out from the joy of houseplants even if you barely see sunny days where you live. From finding out all about my favorite 15 low-light indoor plants to learning some expert care tips for them, you can now bring some gorgeous green buddies to the loving shade of your own home.

But no matter where you keep your houseplants, be it indoors or outdoors, there's one threat that follows them everywhere: bugs and pests! That's what the next chapter is all about, where you'll learn how to identify them and protect your plants effectively!

9

GETTING RID OF BUGS & PESTS

From mealybugs, spider mites, to aphids, bugs and pests are one of the most common challenges that houseplants face around the world. If you're planning to become a (better) plant parent and don't know much about this area of plant care, this chapter has all the golden nuggets to tell you all you need to know. From understanding where these annoying little things come from and preventing them, to learning some tried and true ways to get rid of them — the aim is to help you build and apply some foundational knowledge of pest control. Let's start!

DEALING WITH BUGS AND PESTS

Indoor Plants and Pests

Do indoor plants attract bugs?

If you don't have much experience with houseplants, you might have been of the opinion that plants are safe from pests indoors. That's not the case, though. While the type of pests your plant attracts can vary based on whether it's inside or outside, it can still attract bothersome bugs and pests either way. Aphids is one pest type that you've always got to worry about regardless of where you position your houseplants.

Where do the bugs come from?

The most common pests that you need to look out for in the case of indoor plants are fungus gnats, spider mites, aphids, scale, thrips, whitefly, and mealybugs.

Well, the logical question is ***where do these bugs come from***? You have a clean home and sure enough, you don't see any bugs or pests crawling around your floors so how come they just randomly show up on your indoor plants one day?

Firstly, if you've brought your plants indoors after letting them enjoy their spring and summer outside, that's where most of your suspicion should rest. But that's not the only possibility. Plants that stay indoors all-year round can still get infested. Since these pests are so tiny, there are many ways in which they can sneak in unnoticed. From the fresh produce that you bring into your home to the open windows and doors, there are quite a few channels that could be helping these plant-eaters cross the border. Even your soil mix bags could become a breeding ground for these pests as some bugs like to lay their eggs in soil!

It's important to wash your fresh produce thoroughly as soon as you bring it in, and store your soil in an airtight container to keep pests out instead of helping them multiply!

Prevention Tips

To state the obvious, the best possible way to deal with a plant bug problem is to not let it occur in the first place. Here are a few valuable tips that can help you prevent a pest infestation to save your precious plants from slowly being eaten away!

- Bugs can find their way into your residence through the new plants you bring in. They could already have infested it in the nursery and won't take long before they spread out to your healthy plants at home. To avoid this, make sure you take a close look at new plants and inspect them for pests before bringing them in.
- To prevent the spread of bugs and pests in your houseplants, you should always maintain a healthy amount of space and sufficient airflow between them. Feel free to group them together in an arrangement as long as there's at least a few inches of space between the foliage and pots.
- Practice regular pruning to get rid of all the diseased and dead leaves on your plants. The sooner you do that, the lower the chances of it becoming a breeding ground

for pests. If it falls down on your soil and starts to decompose, for instance, that's a dream situation for bugs!

- Try not to use an old bag of potting soil whenever you're repotting your houseplants, especially if you forgot to seal it shut or store it in an airtight bag. Not wasting all that soil is tempting, but it's also risky as it could already have insect eggs that are undetectable by the naked eye.

- Every time you water or rotate your plants, try to simultaneously inspect it for insects. This allows you to detect the problem early which improves chances for successful treatment and preventing spread.

- God forbid this happens, but if you still do end up noticing an insect or two on one or more of your plants, quarantine it immediately. Move it to an isolated location to avoid infecting any healthy plants neighboring it. Then begin treatment asap with a method that applies to the situation (see below). Which brings us to our next heading — controlling infestation.

How To Control Infestation

There are chemical and non-chemical ways to control a pest infestation in plants. Here are some of the tactics you can apply to your plants under each of the two approaches. It's best to try the non-chemical techniques first, and if all else fails, move on to the tips in the chemical control section.

Non-chemical control tips	Chemical control tips
If an individual section of the plant is infested with pests, destroy the affected area(s). If the root itself is infested, your best bet would be to take a healthy cutting and propagate it.	If the non-chemical solutions don't work and you don't want to discard the plant, you can try out stronger pesticides. Identify the type of pest you're dealing with and ask your local nursery for an appropriate pesticide to tackle it.
Try handpicking with gloves on to treat an early infestation.	Alternate between more than one type of pesticide at each application since some pests are quick to develop a resistance.
Spray the plant with insecticidal soap.	Be sure to check the pesticide's packaging to see if it's labeled for use indoors, since only a few pesticides are.
Wipe off insects using a cotton swab dipped in rubbing alcohol. If they're scale insects, you might have to use your fingernails to scratch them off.	If the type of pesticide you're using requires you to take the plant outside, make sure you do so when the weather is mild. Bring the plant inside when the pesticide dries off completely.
In case of late detection, if your plant seems severely damaged by the pest infestation, it might be best to discard the plant (alongwith its soil) and start fresh.	Be sure to read the "how to use" and "precautions" on the label very carefully before using any chemical pesticide on your houseplant.

FOOLPROOF (DIY) SOLUTIONS TO BEAT HOUSEPLANT PESTS

1. Castile Soap Solution

You can easily make castile soap insecticide at home. It's super effective and much safer to use than a lazy mixture made with dish soap.

All you've got to do is:

1. Find a spray bottle. If you have one that's used, wash and clean it thoroughly it'll work.
2. Mix one tablespoon of liquid castile soap (preferably unscented) for every quart (i.e. 4 cups) of water.
3. Shake well — and it's ready to use!

You can either only spray the affected area or the entire plant (because you never know, right?). The safer route, however, would be to first coat only one leaf with your solution and wait 24 hours to see if there are any signs of damage. If not, feel free to spray the whole thing.

2. Neem Oil

This next solution is completely organic, making it awesome for plants, family-safe, and pet-safe. It can help control a variety of plant pests breeds whether they're eggs, larvae, or adult bugs.

To make your neem oil spray, you'll need a large bucket, a spray bottle (again), and some neem oil extract and liquid castile soap — both of which you can easily find on Amazon.

But what kind of neem oil extract, you might ask? I'd suggest finding something pure and organic, and it's best if you can find it in a cold pressed variety since *Azadirachtin* — the active ingredient, is stronger in those. You'll also need an emulsifier because as can probably recall from science class, oil and water don't mix. The liquid castile soap should fix that. The right quantities for these ingredients for a 2% insecticide would be 10 liters of water, 200 ml neem oil, and 30 ml liquid castile soap.

You can adjust the quantity as long as you maintain the same ratio depending on how many plants you're treating and how much of it you'll need.

Here's what you need to do:

1. Pour your water into a container and add the liquid castile soap.
2. Pour your neem oil in slowly while stirring constantly to get it all mixed well together.
3. Once the mixture is dissolved well, fill your spray bottle with it and shake well before use. Try to use it right away on your plants as the mix only stays good for about 8 hours before starting to lose potency. Drench your plants in it for best results!

3. Pyrethrum Spray

Next we have the pyrethrum spray. It's another key tool to have in your arsenal in the war against houseplant pests. Since you probably haven't heard of this one before, it's pronounced "pie-wreath-rum" and should not be confused with permethrin spray. While permethrin is also used for pest control, it targets mosquitoes, bed bugs, and other insects around the home — not the ones eating your plants alive!

While this type of contact poison is organic, it's not very long-lasting. Factors like exposure to UV light and high temperatures can accelerate pyrethrum's loss of potency. That's why it's best used in cold conditions like applying it overnight.

It's great for indoor use, but that doesn't mean you should also sprinkle your garden with it. Nope! It'll also kill all the beneficial insects out there, including the honey bee which is already an endangered species. The spray won't discriminate between plant-eaters and the good ones — it's toxic to all insects alike.

If your plant collection already has some flowers from the Tanacetum or chrysanthemums family, you can also make this spray at home.

Wear gloves and pick out the flower heads, then leave them to dry out in a dark, cool place. Grind them down until you achieve a coarse texture. As for proportions, 1 cup of this powder should be dissolved in about 2 liters of warm water before being left to stand for several hours. Drain the mixture until there's just water left. Add a teaspoon of cooking oil and liquid castile soap to the mix, and the spray is ready for battle.

Apply it to your indoor plants generously!

The simpler way, however, is to just buy it off the shelf. Read and follow the instructions on the back and use it carefully!

4. Alcohol

Alcohol can also be one of your greatest allies when you're trying to fight back plant pests. There are three types of it including Isopropyl, Ethanol, and Methanol.

The first one, Isopropyl, is also called rubbing alcohol and it's widely available in stores. The concentration on these products can be 70% which is high enough to have antiseptic properties.

Ethanol and methanol, however, will stunt and encourage plant growth respectively. In some concentrations (like 25% or higher for ethanol alcohol), they can even prove to be dangerous or fatal for some plants. So, I'd suggest sticking to isopropyl. It not only helps you solve your pest problem, but can also be used to sterilize your pruning shears or scissors, as well as general cleaning around the house. It's super cheap too!

For pest control, just dip a cotton swab in it and dab on top of your plants. The pests won't like it one bit, especially if you've got mealybugs at hand.

If you're not a fan of dabbing away individual bugs, you can also create a rubbing alcohol spray by diluting it. For every quart (four cups) of water, use one or two cups of 70% rubbing alcohol and mix well.

5. Garlic Spray

Using garlic spray on your houseplants' foliage is a highly effective remedy for getting rid of bugs. You can also use garlic water instead of regular water for a couple of waterings to kill two birds with one stone, i.e. ridding your plant of fungus gnats and nematode problems at the same time.

To make the garlic-based solution, you will need:

1. 1 garlic head
2. A blender or food processor
3. A big jar
4. A large container
5. A Spray bottle

Steps

1. Blend the garlic until the consistency is smooth.
2. Add two cups of water.
3. Pulse the mixture well in your blender or processor.
4. Pour it out into a jar, covering it and letting it sit in a cool, dark place for 24 hours.
5. Strain the mixture as you pour it out into a bigger container and top it up with water until it's filled up to the 1 gallon mark. You can also make less of it as long as you adjust the proportions accordingly.
6. That's it, the garlic solution is ready! Fill it up in your spray bottle and spray the bugs away!

Keep applying this garlic mix to your plants until the pests are all gone.

Herbs You Can Grow Indoors That Are Fly and Bug Repellants

Bugs hate the smells that can seem pleasant to us! You know how rosemary plants can keep flies and mosquitoes away? Mint plays a similar role when it comes to plant bugs. These plants aren't as fast to act as some of the other solutions listed earlier, but it's good to have their scent around the house as an additional layer of protection that keeps the pests away.

6. Just Use Water and a Garden Hose

Ah yes, the gold method of flushing away the pests off your plants. Quite literally.

Simply take your plant outside and give it a shower with the strong jet spray you can find (and that it can handle). As crazy as it sounds, it's actually a pretty promising way of washing bugs away and it works especially well if your indoor plant has become infested with aphids.

Giving your plants a shower can also have a similar effect, though not with the same efficacy.

7. Use Apple Cider Vinegar To Deal With Gnats

Gnats are annoying. But luckily, they're also pretty stupid. The adult ones will literally drown themselves to death if you set the bait for it. All it takes is a bowl filled with apple cider vinegar to attract them.

Cover it up with some cling wrap and pierce some holes through with a fork. They'll crawl in, but won't be able to crawl back out — inevitably drawing to their death.

Sure, the problem won't be completely eliminated since there'll still be eggs and larvae in the soil. But, that should already have been dealt with if you consistently follow this next tip!

8. Diatomaceous Earth

You can use food-grade Diatomaceous Earth as a lethal weapon against bugs in your soil. It can kill any insect that comes into contact with it. Just fill up a plastic soda bottle with it and poke a few holes in the cap. Give it a little squeeze and it'll puff out the powder to easily coat your plants. You'd not only be saving your plant, but also the planet by recycling used plastics!

Add some water to the top soil with each watering and any insect eggs or larvae shouldn't survive — not long enough to develop wings any way.

9. Nematodes

If all else fails, it's time to nuke the bugs with nematodes. Yep, this is where things get nasty.

There are good and bad nematodes, and you can make use of the former for some excellent pest control. Farmers use these regularly and there's no reason why you shouldn't for your indoor houseplants.

None of them are frogs — just little roundworms. These eat all those annoying plant-eating pests for breakfast, giving you some sweet vengeance, and your plants some much-needed relief. The best part? The worms even help fertilize the soil after every meal (ahem) — leaving your plant more nourished. Can't get much better than that, can it?

CONCLUSION

And that brings us to the end of this indoor plant bible! Phew, what a journey it's been. From desk plants to poisonous ones, watering to propagation, and low-light plants to succulents — this book has covered everything you need to know about indoor plants in grave detail.

Hopefully, you now have not just a better understanding, but also an appreciation of the overwhelming amount of benefits plants can offer us in our day-to-day lives. You also know which ones are toxic and whether or not you need to be careful with their placement around the house. Plus, with all the propagation hacks shared in this book, I'm hoping that the only money you spend on houseplants is on your very first cutting of each new species you adopt.

The plant-specific propagation techniques, methods, and steps shared in this book should be enough to multiply plants for not just your own needs, but also your friends' and family's! Sure, you probably don't remember much of it off the back of your head, but that's the beauty of it — you can keep coming back to this as a handbook of all the facts and info you need, whenever you need it!

If you're reading this, then I'm so glad that you made it through this entire book. It shows how passionate you are about this new hobby and you actually want to get good at it. Well, now that you've accumulated my decade's worth of knowledge, it's time to start applying some of it one step at a time! Grab a cutting of some of your favorite houseplants and start growing some healthy, gorgeous little guys!

And I genuinely love hearing success stories from my readers and it's one of the biggest motivators for me to keep creating more content like this. So, if you do find the information useful and end up applying some propagation or pest control hacks shared here, **please do tell me the story through a review on Amazon**. I read through every single one of those!

Speaking of Amazon, you can also check out my first book titled "Indoor Plant Care 101" over there — it's a must-read if you want to expand your knowledge of indoor plants even further!

Finally, thank you from the bottom of my beating heart for reading my book. I wish you the best of luck in all your planting endeavors.

- Goodbye!

REFERENCES

Prestigious Plantscapes. (n.d.). 9 Surprising Facts About Indoor Plants. Retrieved from https://www.prestigiousplantscapes.com.au/9-surprising-facts-about-indoor-plants/

Costa Farms. (n.d.). 12 Things You Did Not Know About Houseplants. Retrieved from https://costafarms.com/blogs/get-growing/12-things-you-did-not-know-about-houseplants

MyJournalCourier.com. (n.d.). Home: Houseplants for Busy People. Retrieved from https://www.myjournalcourier.com/news/article/home-house plants-for-busy-people-17403685.php

Rania El-Tanbouly, Ziad Hassan, & Sarah El-Messeiry (2021). Effects of Indoor Plants on Human Health: A Systematic Review. Frontiers in Molecular Biosciences. Reetrieved from https://www.frontiersin.org/arti cles/10.3389/fmolb.2021.709395/full

Bloomscape. (n.d.). Office Plants: Lower Stress, Improve Concentration. Retrieved from https://bloomscape.com/green-living/office-plants-lower-stress-improve-concentration/

Patch. (n.d.). How to Propagate Houseplants. Retrieved from https://www. patchplants.com/gb/en/read/plant-care/how-to-propagate-houseplants/

Better Homes & Gardens. (n.d.). Propagating Houseplants. Retrieved from https://www.bhg.com/gardening/houseplants/care/propagating-houseplants/

House Plants Expert. (n.d.). Propagating House Plants. Retrieved from https://www.houseplantsexpert.com/propagating-house-plants.html

Christensen, D. (n.d.). How to Propagate Houseplants: Air Layering and Simple Layering. Iowa State University Extension and Outreach. Retrieved from https://hortnews.extension.iastate.edu/how-propagate-houseplants-air-layering-and-simple-layering

Gardening Know How. (n.d.). Propagating Houseplant Seeds: Tips For Growing Houseplant Seeds Retrieved from https://www.gardening knowhow.com/houseplants/hpgen/propagating-houseplant-seeds.htm

Gardeners' World Magazine. (n.d.). Six Propagation Mistakes to Avoid.

Retrieved from https://www.gardenersworld.com/how-to/grow-plants/six-propagation-mi stakes-to-avoid/

Apartment Therapy. (n.d.). How to Propagate Plants: Weekend Projects. Retrieved from https://www.apartmenttherapy.com/how-to-propagate-plants-weekend-projects-258823

Better Homes & Gardens. (n.d.). Tough Houseplants: Our Top Picks. Retrieved from https://www.bhg.com/gardening/houseplants/care/tough-houseplants/

University of Missouri Extension. (2021). Houseplants: Selection and Care (G6560). Retrieved from https://extension.missouri.edu/publications/g6560

Thursd. (n.d.). Top 10 Most Wanted Rare Houseplants. Retrieved from https://thursd.com/posts/top-10-most-wanted-rare-houseplants

Sprouts and Stems. (n.d.). Anthurium Veitchii: Velvet Cardboard Anthurium Care Guide. Retrieved from https://sproutsandstems.com/anthurium-veitchii/

Garden Betty. (n.d.). Philodendron Erubescens 'Pink Princess': Growing Tips and Care Guide. Retrieved from https://www.gardenbetty.com/philodendron-erubescens-pink-princess/

Choi, W. S., Chun, J. H., & Lee, Y. W. (2010). Evaluation of Anti-Inflammatory, Anti-Tumor, and Anti-Allergic Activities of the Ethanol Extract of Anthurium andraeanum. Planta Medica, 76(6), 605-611. https://doi:10.1055/s-0029-1240629

Our House Plants. (n.d.). Poisonous Houseplants - Which Indoor Plants Are Toxic and Dangerous? Retrieved from https://www.ourhouseplants.com/guides/poisonous-houseplants

Better Homes & Gardens. (n.d.). Poisonous Houseplants: 10 Indoor Plants for Pet Owners and Parents to Avoid. Retrieved from https://www.bhg.com/gardening/houseplants/projects/poisonous-houseplants/

Earthbath. (n.d.). Three Pet Safety Tips for Plant People. Retrieved from https://www.earthbath.com/blogs/earthbath-blog/three-pet-safety-tips-for-plant-people

Our House Plants. (n.d.). Poisonous Houseplants - Which Indoor Plants Are Toxic and Dangerous? Retrieved from https://www.ourhouseplants.com/guides/poisonous-houseplants

Faust Island. (n.d.). Houseplant Safety for Children - Keep Your Child Safe

From Poisoning. Retrieved from https://www.faustisland.com/house plant-safety-for-children/

Our House Plants. (n.d.). Poisonous Houseplants - Which Indoor Plants Are Toxic and Dangerous? Retrieved from https://www.ourhouseplants.com/ guides/poisonous-houseplants

Better Homes & Gardens. (n.d.). Poisonous Houseplants: 10 Indoor Plants for Pet Owners and Parents to Avoid. Retrieved from https://www.bhg.com/ gardening/houseplants/projects/poisonous-housepla nts/

Earthbath. (n.d.). Three Pet Safety Tips for Plant People. Retrieved from https://www.earthbath.com/blogs/earthbath-blog/three-pet-safety-tips-for-plant-people

Our House Plants. (n.d.). Poisonous Houseplants - Which Indoor Plants Are Toxic and Dangerous? Retrieved from https://www.ourhouseplants.com/ guides/poisonous-houseplants

Faust Island. (n.d.). Houseplant Safety for Children - Keep Your Child Safe From Poisoning. Retrieved from https://www.faustisland.com/house plant-safety-for-children/

House Beautiful. (n.d.). 15 Interesting Facts About Succulents. Retrieved from https://www.housebeautiful.com/lifestyle/gardening/g3441/interesting-facts-about-succulents/

PureWow. (n.d.). The 25 Types of Succulents You Need to Know. Retrieved from https://www.purewow.com/home/types-of-succulents

HGTV. (n.d.). 10 Secrets for Growing Succulents. Retrieved from https:// www.hgtv.com/outdoors/flowers-and-plants/10-secrets-for-super-succu lents-pictures

The Spruce. (n.d.). How to Make a Succulent Container Garden. Retrieved from https://www.thespruce.com/make-a-succulent-plant-container-garden-848006

Country Living. (n.d.). How to Plant a Succulent Garden in a Bowl. Retrieved from https://www.countryliving.com/gardening/garden-ideas/how-to/ a4992/plant-a-succulent-garden-in-a-bowl/

Reader's Digest. (n.d.). 15 Low-Light Houseplants That Thrive in Near Darkness. Retrieved from https://www.rd.com/list/low-light-houseplants/

Melinda Myers. (n.d.). Caring for Indoor Plants in Low-Light Conditions. Retrieved from https://www.melindamyers.com/audio-video/melindas-

garden-moment-audio-tips/houseplants-holiday-plants-cut-flowers/
caring-for-indoor-plants-in-low-light-conditions

Architectural Digest. (n.d.). Caring for Indoor Plants in Low-Light Conditions. Retrieved from https://www.architecturaldigest.com/story/caring-for-indoor-plants-in-low-light-conditions

Smart Garden Guide. (n.d.). Do Indoor Plants Attract Bugs? Retrieved from https://smartgardenguide.com/do-indoor-plants-attract-bugs/

Get Busy Gardening. (n.d.). Where Do Houseplant Pests Come From? Retrieved from https://getbusygardening.com/where-do-houseplant-pests-come-from/

Clemson Cooperative Extension Home & Garden Information Center. (2020). Common Houseplant Insects and Related Pests. Retrieved from https://hgic.clemson.edu/factsheet/common-houseplant-insects-related-pests/

The Practical Planter. (n.d.). How to Get Rid of Bugs on Indoor Plants. Retrieved from https://thepracticalplanter.com/how-to-get-rid-of-bugs-on-indoor-plants/

Pestech Pest Solutions. (n.d.). Pest Repelling Houseplants: The Ultimate Guide. Retrieved from https://pestech.com/blog/pest-repelling-houseplants/

Andermatt Garden. (n.d.). Nematodes Guide: What Are They and How to Use Them? Retrieved from https://andermattgarden.co.uk/blogs/articles/nematodes-guide/

West Virginia University Extension Service. (2021, March 1). How Plants Use Water. Retrieved from https://extension.wvu.edu/lawn-gardening-pests/news/2021/03/01/how-plants-use-water

Rural Sprout. (n.d.). Houseplant Watering Hacks: 11 Simple Tricks for Happy Plants. Retrieved from https://www.ruralsprout.com/houseplant-watering-hacks/

Garden Betty. (n.d.). Spring Cleaning Tip: Don't Forget to Shower Your Houseplants! Retrieved from https://www.gardenbetty.com/spring-cleaning-tip-dont-forget-to-shower-your-houseplants/

Balcony Garden Web. (n.d.). How to Water Plants While Away: 6 Brilliant Hacks. Retrieved from https://balconygardenweb.com/how-to-water-plants-while-away-6-brilliant-hacks/

ProFlowers. (n.d.). How to Water Plants While Away: 6 DIY Methods. Retrieved from https://www.proflowers.com/blog/how-to-water-plants-while-away

Plantician. (n.d.). What Does a Plant Sitter Do? Retrieved from https://www.plantician.com/what-does-a-plant-sitter-do/

Wild Interiors. (n.d.). Hire a Plant Sitter for Your Indoor Garden. Retrieved from https://www.wildinteriors.com/blog/hire-a-plant-sitter

Made in the USA
Las Vegas, NV
13 December 2023

82726186R00105